COME FOR REFUGE

The book of Ruth and hope for migrants

AN ESSENTIAL STUDY GUIDE FOR INDIVIDUALS AND CHURCHES

PETE WILCOX

BRF
Ministries

'*Come for Refuge* is a story of our time and a story of all times. Resonating with profound relevance, it weaves first-hand accounts of refugees today with those of biblical characters, reminding us that themes of migration, refuge, and asylum are nothing new. There is a potency in the dialogue between contemporary voices and ancient text, each illuminating and enhancing the other, and together revealing that amid pain and tragedy there is also light and hope.'
The Rt Revd Dr Guli Francis-Dehqani, bishop of Chelmsford

'This brilliant book provides a rich comparison of the experiences of migrants now to the challenges of Naomi and Ruth. In a world where hostility to migrants is on the rise, Bishop Pete shows us the striking themes and similarities in journeys between Ruth and Naomi and modern migrants. The case studies highlight the desperate challenges but also the route to belonging that many migrants follow. It paints a vivid picture of the necessity of movement of people, from famine, loss, and persecution to returning home and the equal necessity for us to welcome and show understanding to our migrant communities.'
Olivia Blake, MP for Sheffield, Hallam

'Living in cities with significant migrant communities in London, and now in Melbourne, I have seen both the deep gifts migrants bring and the profound vulnerabilities they carry. Pete Wilcox names these realities in this beautiful book with honesty and grace, challenging church and society alike to respond not with fear, but with love, compassion, and faithful welcome. *Come for Refuge* deserves to be widely read, studied, and shared!'
The Most Revd Ric Thorpe, archbishop of Melbourne

Ministries

15 The Chambers, Vineyard
Abingdon OX14 3FE
+44(0)1865 319700 | brf.org.uk

Bible Reading Fellowship (BRF) is a charity (233280)
and company limited by guarantee (301324), registered in England and Wales

EU Authorised Representative: Easy Access System Europe – Mustamäe tee 50,
10621 Tallinn, Estonia, gpsr.requests@easproject.com

ISBN 978 1 80039 549 7
First published 2026
10 9 8 7 6 5 4 3 2 1 0

A catalogue record for this book is available from the British Library

Printed and bound by CPI Group (UK) Ltd, Croydon CR0 4YY

CONTENTS

ACT IV: INTEGRATION AND INHERITANCE

EPILOGUE: CONTRIBUTION AND LEGACY

Introduction

The book of Ruth and contemporary migration stories

The book of Ruth is the story not just of one woman, but of two: Ruth and Naomi. The whole narrative is only four chapters long: Naomi is most prominent in chapters 1 and 4 (though Ruth is present), and Ruth is most prominent in chapters 2 and 3 (though Naomi is present). Both women had experience of migration: Naomi was an Israelite who went to live as a migrant in the land of Moab; Ruth was a Moabite who went to live as a migrant in the land of Israel. For Naomi, migration was essentially a bitter experience; for Ruth, a much more fulfilling one – she sought and found refuge (the word is used of her in 2:12) in Bethlehem and almost certainly never returned to her country of origin.

This exposition of the book of Ruth seeks to pay particular attention to those experiences of migration. I would argue that the text invites this focus, not least by the way in which it repeatedly places stress on Ruth's migrant status: again and again, sometimes gratuitously, she is 'Ruth the Moabite' (1:4, 22; 2:2, 21; 4:5, 10) and once she is 'the Moabite… from the country of Moab' (2:6). Once she describes herself as 'a foreigner' (2:10) – in Hebrew, *nākerîyāh*, an alien.

However, my sensitivity to this emphasis in the book of Ruth has been heightened by my recent interactions with migrants and refugees in the two cities in the UK in which I have lived in the last twelve years: specifically with refugees and asylum seekers from Iran (and Kurdistan) in Liverpool and with refugees from Ukraine in Sheffield. Their stories of leaving a beloved homeland, of risk-laden journeys, of uncertain and uneven welcomes in a new and deeply unfamiliar country have enriched (among other things) my reading of this biblical text.

That enrichment is what has prompted me to experiment with the format in this book. I have tried to create a conversation between the experience of Ruth and Naomi, on the one hand, and that of some contemporary migrants, refugees, and asylum seekers, on the other. I am deeply grateful to those individuals who have confided their stories in me and who have trusted me to place their testimonies alongside the Bible story. How far this experiment is a success will be for others to judge, but I am immensely grateful to those whose risky frankness with me made the experiment possible. I am especially thankful to those who provided me with testimonies which, on account of various inevitable editorial considerations, I have not ultimately been able to include in this book. Their generosity, patience, grace, and understanding have been exemplary.

These testimonies are drawn from two contexts: Sheffield, in England, where I serve as bishop of the Anglican diocese; and Melbourne, Australia, where I drafted much of this book during a sabbatical.

As the bishop of Sheffield, it is my privilege to be one of the patrons of a magnificent charity called ASSIST, which seeks to support some of the most vulnerable people in our City of Sanctuary. So it was an obvious step, not least as a way of drawing attention to the extraordinary work of the staff and volunteers of ASSIST, to seek to secure some of these testimonies from among those the charity has supported – though not all the 'Sheffield' stories are 'ASSIST' stories.

Part of the point of this book is to underline the fact that migration is a global challenge requiring a global response. Our experience of increased migration to the UK in recent decades is by no means unique – quite the opposite. On sabbatical, I had barely been in Melbourne for 48 hours before I became aware of the extent of migration to that city at present and of the work of the Anglican Church in seeking to support asylum seekers, refugees, and other migrants there. The opportunity to include testimonies from migrants to Melbourne seemed, in the providence of God, too good to miss, and I am delighted that it has proved possible.

The challenge of rising global migration and government policy

Migration has been growing globally for decades. The *World Migration Report* for 2024, published by the United Nations' International Organization for Migration (IOM), estimates that 'there are about 281 million international migrants in the world, which equates to 3.6 per cent of the global population'. It goes on to state that this number is '128 million more than 30 years earlier, in 1990 (153 million), and over three times the estimated number in 1970 (84 million)'.[1]

Some definitions will be useful at this point, and I have been working with those offered by the IOM. It uses the word 'migrant' as an umbrella term with the broadest possible scope, to refer to any person who for any reason now lives in a country other than the country of their birth. In this sense students studying overseas, for example, are migrants. According to the 1951 Convention relating to the Status of Refugees, cited by the IOM, the term 'refugee' has a much narrower meaning. It refers to 'persons who, owing to a well-founded fear of persecution for reasons of race, religion, nationality, membership of a particular social group or political opinion, are outside the country of their nationality and are unable or, owing to such fear, are unwilling to avail themselves of the protection of that country'.[2] Thirdly, again using the IOM definition, an asylum seeker is 'someone whose claim has not yet been finally decided on by the country in which he or she has submitted it. Not every asylum seeker will ultimately be recognized as a refugee, but every recognized refugee is initially an asylum seeker'.[3]

Every refugee and asylum seeker is therefore a migrant, but by no means is every migrant a refugee or asylum seeker. Migrants may be relatively prosperous and may exercise substantial freedom of choice and agency in making a migration. Obviously, however, there are also many migrants who are not prosperous and who have little freedom of choice or agency when they migrate; they might best be described as 'forced migrants'. These include increasing numbers of trafficked persons and increasing numbers of climate migrants (seeking to escape famine and drought, for example), as well as migrants who are fleeing conflict or war. The testimonies of contemporary migrants in this book are exclusively those of refugees and asylum seekers – of migrants who have found themselves in vulnerable situations. Although 'forced migrants' is not a happy phrase, and not a universally accepted one, I use it to emphasise the vulnerability, not least, of Ruth in the Bible story.

It is interesting to note that the IOM has an essentially positive disposition towards the phenomenon of migration, even towards globally increasing migration, seeing it as part of the solution to the world's great problems, rather than as a contributor to them. In its 'Institutional Strategy on Migration and Sustainable Development', the IOM argues that 'migration, when well managed, can be both a development strategy and a development outcome', contributing to, rather than hindering, the achievement of the UN's sustainable development goals. It notes, for example, that many migrants are economically productive and benefit not only their country of residence but their country of origin, too.[4] The IOM estimates that 'remittances' (financial or in-kind transfers made by migrants directly to families or communities in their countries of origin) increased from US$128 billion in 2000 to US$831 billion in 2022.[5] Of course, what migrants contribute to both their country of residence and their country of origin should not be measured purely financially.

This rather positive stance towards global migration is noticeably at odds with recent government policy in the UK. For well over a decade, until July 2024, the Conservative government sought to respond to (indeed, to combat) increasing migration by the creation of a so-called 'hostile environment' – 'a range of measures aimed at identifying and reducing the number of immigrants in the UK with no right to remain', which by 2018 had shockingly led to the wrongful deportation of at least 63 members of the Windrush generation.[6] Although the terminology was generally abandoned latterly (in favour of 'a compliant environment'), the policy has not. Thus during 2023, the government introduced the Illegal Migration Act (designed not least to 'stop the boats' crossing the English Channel) and procured the Bibby Stockholm accommodation barge as a holding centre for asylum seekers awaiting the outcome of their claims. A treaty with Rwanda was also signed in December that year, with the associated legislation placed before Parliament in 2024, to enable asylum seekers to be removed there. Only the general election in July 2024 and the consequential change of government prevented the passage of the Rwanda legislation and the implementation of the treaty. Those measures were all highly controversial: indeed, the earliest attempt to arrange the deportation of asylum seekers in the UK to Rwanda was ruled unlawful by the UK's own Supreme Court in December 2022. However, if it had been expected that the election of a Labour government would mean a clear policy shift in a more humane direction, those hopes have not been realised – on the contrary, the 2025 'Border Security, Asylum, and Immigration Act' actually represents 'more of the same'.

Of course, hard cases make bad law, and the book of Ruth is not a policy document. It goes without saying that it is neither possible nor appropriate to extrapolate from the experience of two individuals in a setting over 2,000 miles from Britain and over 3,000 years ago to contemporary national government policy. However, national government policy becomes inhumane precisely when it loses sight of its impact on individual migrants. So the book of Ruth may nevertheless helpfully encourage us to reflect on what good government policy can look like and what kind of outcomes it might enable.

To assist in such reflection, this book includes study materials, primarily designed for group use but also capable of being used by individuals. There are study materials to accompany each of the six main chapters of the book, each set including questions both about the biblical text and about the experience of contemporary migrants, as well as suggestions for worship and for further activity.

The structure of the book of Ruth and migration

While holy scripture is, of course, always more than carefully crafted literature, it is seldom less than that, and the artfully composed book of Ruth is a case in point. It has a clear and deliberate structure: it is a 'chiasm'.

A chiasm is a literary device, common in Hebrew biblical literature, in which a text has a symmetrical shape: ABC in the first half of a text is followed by its reflection, C'B'A', in the second. In the case of the book of Ruth, in the first half of the chiasm, a report of the demise of a family line (A) is followed by an account of Naomi's emptiness (B), which is in turn followed by a story about Ruth and Boaz in a harvest field (C). Then in the mirror image of the chiasm, a story about Boaz and Ruth on a threshing-floor (C') is followed by an account of Naomi's fullness (B'), which is in turn followed by a genealogy charting the renewal of a family line (A'). It can be depicted as follows:

A	Prologue (1:1–5): the demise of a family line
B	Act I (1:6–22): Naomi's emptiness
C	Act II (2:1–23): Ruth and Boaz, part 1
C'	Act III (3:1–18): Ruth and Boaz, part 2
B'	Act IV (4:1–17): Naomi's fullness
A'	Epilogue (4:18–22): the renewal of a family line

In the ensuing pages, the six chapters expound each of the six parts of the chiasm in turn. The intention has been to stay close to the biblical text, respecting its contours, its shape, and its structure. What is offered is a literary and theological reading, which takes the text at face value and pays attention to word plays and semantic patterns. Like any short story, the text of the book of Ruth has to be taken at face value, in order to appropriate its meaning. It has to be read realistically – or indeed heard realistically. (Over the centuries it is likely that the book of Ruth has had as many hearers as readers. I tend therefore to refer to the audience of the book rather than its readers.) Elements of the interpretation are inevitably speculative, a reading between the lines, but the aim on such occasions has always been to enable the biblical text to have its full dramatic impact.

The six parts of the chiasm together relate the happy reversal of fortune experienced by Naomi and Ruth. As such, the six parts describe a journey which contemporary migrants are often hoping to follow: from an initial crisis and calamity to a migration which often calls kinship into question, through a period of subsistence and heightened vulnerability, to a more settled situation of security and wellbeing, to eventual integration and inheritance, and finally to contribution and legacy. This scheme maps onto the chiasm as follows:

Prologue: Crisis and calamity – the demise of a family line
    Act I: Migration and kinship – Naomi's emptiness
        Act II: Subsistence and vulnerability – Ruth and Boaz in the field
        Act III: Security and wellbeing – Ruth and Boaz on the threshing-floor
    Act IV: Integration and inheritance – Naomi's fullness
Epilogue: Contribution and legacy – the renewal of a family line

Readers of this book may also discern that this scheme has informed the way in which the testimonies of contemporary migrants have been interwoven with the biblical exposition.

To assist the reader to engage directly with the biblical text, it has been printed together with the commentary, scene by scene. The translation is the Anglicised NRSVue – chosen for the balance it achieves between a closeness to the Hebrew text, on the one hand, and a fluency of contemporary English, on the other.

Victor's story

to Sheffield from Zimbabwe

Victor's story has been included first as something of a paradigm. It illustrates the whole migrant journey, from crisis and calamity, to migration and kinship, to subsistence and vulnerability, to security and wellbeing, to integration and inheritance, and finally to contribution and legacy.

My name is Victor Mujakachi. I was born in Zimbabwe (formerly Rhodesia) 64 years ago. Southern Rhodesia was a British colony, which became a self-governing colony in 1923. Rhodesia declared independence in 1965, triggering civil disorder between the white minority government and the large black majority, which escalated into a 15-year civil war. This ended in 1980 with a political settlement brokered by the British government and the establishment of modern Zimbabwe, governed by its indigenous black majority.

For the first 20 years of my life, I lived under a form of apartheid. Even at primary school, I was aware of the injustice. Society was divided into three spheres: white, Asian, and black. We lived in separate residential areas, used separate shops, restaurants and public transport systems, and were educated in separate schools. We even worshipped in separate churches.

In my teens, I became more politically aware. During the 1960s and 70s unrest grew, orchestrated by black activists and guerilla fighters coming over from countries such as Zambia, Tanzania, and Malawi, from which they had moved to join the armed struggle against the Rhodesian government.

As a young person, I was strongly pro-nationalist and planned to join those fighting for the cause of black people in Rhodesia. However, a cousin who planned to help me join the insurgency in Zambia was arrested and executed, so for a time my involvement was subdued.

Yet momentum for change was irresistible. In 1979, Margaret Thatcher initiated discussions with Rhodesian Prime Minister Ian Smith, leading to free elections in 1980 and our country's first democratic government under Robert Mugabe. For me, this meant I could begin a career in our new nation. I was invited to join the police, but moved instead into banking, where I remained for 23 years.

Initially, there was a climate of euphoria and expectation among the black majority, disenfranchised by almost a hundred years of colonisation. Sadly, this period was short-lived. Mugabe began to exert one-party control, suppressing critics and opponents. In 1981, my brother and I, with two other family members, were forcibly taken, interrogated, and beaten by former guerilla fighters for daring to question government policies. This was not the freedom we had sought.

For many years, though, I remained conflicted. I was unhappy with Mugabe's increasingly autocratic rule, constitutional changes, corruption, and repression. But my career was progressing well, and I had high hopes for the 1999 elections. Opposition parties were gaining traction, including the new and popular Movement for Democratic Change. However, after Mugabe instigated a well-documented violent crackdown ahead of the elections, I knew it was time to leave Zimbabwe.

In 2003, I left for the UK with my wife Memory and our three children, on a three-year student visa. By then, the opposition had regained momentum and was expected to defeat Mugabe at the next election. My intention was to return after completing my studies. The UK had been an obvious choice. English was the official language of Zimbabwe and, at the time, Zimbabwe's 'most favoured nation' status meant no visa was required upon entry for visitors. I enrolled in a bachelor's degree, aiming to proceed to postgraduate studies. For a few years family life was settled. We remained hopeful Mugabe would be ousted, after which I'd return to my banking career and contribute to the development of my beloved Zimbabwe. We were so optimistic that Memory continued her job in Zimbabwe at the South African Embassy, visiting me twice a year, while I did the same from here.

The 2008 elections took place soon after Memory had visited me with our youngest child. We were, however, once again disappointed, as Mugabe's ZANU-PF party rigged the election. I wrote to a friend back home, highly critical of the government. Somehow my letter became known to the government and my friend was arrested. Memory lost her job, we believe because of political interference, but she was unable to join me because I claimed asylum while she was still in Zimbabwe.

For the next 14 years, I was forcibly separated from my wife and youngest child. Even when Memory was able to join me in 2022, our younger son could not secure a visa for himself, and so he now lives in China. I saw him again in the summer of 2024, for the first time in nearly 20 years!

When my asylum application was submitted in 2008, I was relocated from my home in London to Sheffield. Here, I made contact with ASSIST, a charity supporting refugees and asylum seekers. My involvement with ASSIST opened up a network of friends who supported me in many different ways, for which I'll be forever grateful.

That support reached its peak when the British government sought to deport me to Zimbabwe in 2019. The Sheffield community stood up for me, and in four days garnered nearly 80,000 signatures petitioning against my deportation. After this massive outcry, the government relented. The support I received is without doubt the most positive experience of my life in the UK. The Sheffield community offered me advice, encouragement, moral support, financial assistance, and a place to live with a host family for twelve of my 14 years as an asylum seeker.

I spent 14 years in the asylum system. I had no right to employment or accommodation, no means of sustenance and limited access to healthcare. Those years were far from easy, with periods of distress, soul-searching, depression, fear, insecurity, anguish, emotional turmoil, and at worst listless resignation. I found life in the UK challenging because of the culture, customs, language – and food! Although Zimbabwe is an English-speaking country, I struggled badly with the different regional accents and colloquialisms. The British weather, which changes very quickly and dramatically, unlike where I come from, often caught me off guard.

Despite all the trials and tribulations of my long asylum journey, I lived within a community who supported me in a massive way. These people empathised with my situation. They gave me strength, encouragement, and assurance in the face of adversity. They gave me hope.

PROLOGUE

CRISIS AND CALAMITY

THE DEMISE OF A FAMILY LINE (RUTH 1:1–5)

The opening (1:1–5) and closing (4:18–22) paragraphs of the book of Ruth, the first and last sections of its symmetrical structure, have much in common with one another. They are the least 'narrative' parts of the book. The many named characters in these two sections are the least fully developed: they don't speak (dialogue is a prominent feature of all the other sections of the book), they barely act, and it is hard to get much sense of their personalities, except in so far as their names provide hints. These are also the only two sections of the book of Ruth in which there is no reference to the Lord. (It will become clear that the distribution of these references through the book as a whole is suggestive.)

Although in themselves these opening and closing sections of Ruth have little narrative content, they do have a definite narrative purpose – to capture the transformation in the circumstances of the family of Elimelech. In the prologue, the family is forced by famine into migration from Israel to Moab. The future is bleak and precarious. The family line appears like it is about to expire. In the epilogue, the family line is secure once again and a most glorious future indicated, culminating in the birth of King David no less. Yet readers who are at least a little familiar with the Hebrew scriptures will recall that even King David will himself become an asylum seeker and refugee, multiple times.

> [1]In the days when the judges ruled, there was a famine in the land, and a certain man of Bethlehem in Judah went to live in the country of Moab, he and his wife and two sons. [2]The name of the man was Elimelech and the name of his wife Naomi, and the names of his two sons were Mahlon and Chilion; they were

Ephrathites from Bethlehem in Judah. They went into the country of Moab and remained there. ³But Elimelech, the husband of Naomi, died, and she was left with her two sons. ⁴These took Moabite wives; the name of the one was Orpah and the name of the other Ruth. When they had lived there for about ten years, ⁵both Mahlon and Chilion also died, so that the woman was left without her two sons and her husband.

RUTH 1:1–5

In this short first scene of the drama, before the first character is ushered on to the stage, two preliminary facts are stated by way of context: the first is historical and the second is socio-economic.

Historically, the story is set 'in the days when the judges ruled'. If nothing else, this accounts for the place the book of Ruth has been given within the Christian Bible: it is sandwiched between Judges itself and 1 Samuel, in which the story of Israel's kingdom is begun. Historians date the period of the judges to about 1100BC, but precision is frankly unnecessary as well as impossible – a precise date would make little difference to a reading of the story.

The book of Judges passes a negative judgement on the life of the people of God at that time: it was a period when 'there was no king in Israel' and 'all the people did what was right in their own eyes' (Judges 21:25). It was a time of extreme social chaos and moral corruption. Some of the most gruesome stories in the Hebrew scriptures are to be found in its pages, many of them stories of macho-violence and what might today be called 'toxic masculinity' – think of Samson, to name only the best known. Many of the narratives in Judges, especially towards the end of the book, include episodes of terrible violence against women. Certainly 'the days when the judges ruled' were days of great vulnerability for women and when kindness towards women (which will prove to be a characteristic feature of the book of Ruth) was in short supply.

Socio-economically, the story is set in a time of famine. The dearth of food in Israel is fundamental to the plot of the book of Ruth because it triggers the migration of an Israelite family. Famine was, of course, a recurring feature of life in ancient Israel – and the economic migration with which the story of Ruth begins recalls the earlier journeyings (mostly to Egypt) of Abraham (Genesis 12:10), Isaac (Genesis 26:1), and Jacob (Genesis 42:5; 43:1; 47:4).

In this instance, it is a certain man of Bethlehem in Judah who is driven from his home in search of food. The name Bethlehem means 'house of bread': if famine has reached even here, then the situation is dire indeed. This man 'went to live in the country of Moab, he and his wife and two sons': the text perhaps implies that it was the man's decision, the man's initiative to migrate. We are offered no insight into what his wife or children thought, whether they were willing participants in this adventure or reluctant ones. Naomi is not the first woman, nor the last, to be made to migrate against her will and against her better judgement.

This Bethlehemite, then, goes with his wife and two sons to live in Moab. Depending on the actual destination, it may have been a journey of as little as 30 miles, but it would have required the family to cross the River Jordan and navigate the Rift Valley. And in any case, Moab is a hostile location. From its very first appearance in the biblical story, Moab is a bad place. Its eponymous ancestor is born in disreputable circumstances (Genesis 19:30–37). It is a kingdom bent at the time of the Exodus on the cursing and destruction of Israel (Numbers 22—24) and on fighting against it (Joshua 24:9). It is viewed by Israel as a place and a people of sexual and spiritual promiscuity and temptation (Numbers 25:1–2; Judges 10:6). Later in history, it is a kingdom which oppressed Israel and from which Israel required deliverance (Judges 3:12–30), an enemy against whom Israel regularly fought (e.g. 1 Samuel 12:9; 14:47; 2 Samuel 8:12; 2 Kings 3:5).

There is, then, something ill-omened about this migration: an Israelite would not lightly choose to journey from Israel to Moab. 'Moab?', the audience is invited to ask, 'Can anything good come out of Moab?' At the very least, the fact that Moab represents an attractive option is an indication of how desperate conditions in Israel must have been.

There is a particular irony in the fact that, at the time of the exodus, when the people of Israel, en route to the promised land, passed through Moabite territory and requested aid (bread and water), they were denied it (Deuteronomy 23:3); now inhospitable Moab commends itself as a place of sanctuary for Elimelech. It cannot have been an easy decision to make this journey, and it probably wasn't an easy journey. Generally, contemporary 'forced' migrants will recognise the difficulty of both.

There is some dramatic emphasis in the fact that the characters who make this journey are not immediately named. In verse 1, we are just told that the story involved 'a certain man… his wife and two sons'. It is only in verse 2 that their names are supplied: the man is Elimelech, his wife is Naomi, and their sons are Mahlon and Chilion. In all four cases, repetitively, the introduction includes the actual word 'name', as it will do again (twice more) in verse 4, when we are given the names of the sons' wives. Names, and also anonymity, are significant throughout this book and not least at its conclusion (see 2:1, 19; 4:5, 10 [x2], 11, 14, 17).

In the man's case and in his wife's, the derivations of their names are straightforward and probably meaningful. Elimelech means 'My God is king' or 'God is my king'. The name may well be a further reminder that in the period of the judges 'there was no king in Israel' (Judges 17:6; 18:1; 19:1; 21:25), while also anticipating the focus on David's royal line with which the book will close. The likelihood of this is increased by the reference to Ephratha and Bethlehem (compare 1 Samuel 17:12). Naomi's name means 'pleasant' or 'sweet' and introduces her as a happy woman. The tragedies that are about to strike befall a woman who has, until this point, known mostly sweetness in her life.

The etymologies of their sons' names are less certain, but both seem ominous. A likely derivation of Mahlon is from the Hebrew word *hala*, meaning 'to be sick', and Chilion is almost certainly derived from the word *kala*, meaning 'to end'.

These four Ephrathites 'went into the country of Moab' and 'sojourned' there (exactly the same word is used with reference to Elimelech here as is used with reference to Abraham in Genesis 12:10). It implies migrant status: a sojourner is not a citizen. It may also imply that the family only envisaged a short-term stay in Moab and hoped to return promptly to Bethlehem. When the text goes on to state that 'they went to Moab and remained there', it may mean their initial expectations were confounded. This too is an experience to which many contemporary refugees can relate: what was at first envisaged as a temporary measure becomes an unimaginably lengthy stay.

The prologue focuses on one family from Bethlehem, but when the opening line tells us that there is a famine in the land, we can infer that the famine affected the whole land of Israel. Indeed, if the famine were not general in the whole land of Israel, no Israelite would choose to migrate to Moab. On the other hand, if the famine did affect the whole land of Israel, it is unlikely that Elimelech was the only one to make this hard decision and to migrate. There must have been others, perhaps even from Bethlehem, left with no choice but to make this challenging journey. Possibly the road from Bethlehem to Moab was well trodden.

The text is silent about the particular challenges Elimelech, Naomi, and their sons encountered as migrants in Moab, especially at first – with respect to language and customs, finding housing and work, making friends and belonging; but those challenges will surely have been there.

A significant shift follows in verse 3. In the first two verses, the story is told, as one might expect, as if Elimelech were the principal character. He is the first character introduced in verse 1 and the first to be named in verse 2. The end of verse 1 further emphasises his priority: the story is about *him* and *his* wife and *his* two sons. Yet although he is also first named in verse 3, the expectations of the audience are then confounded by his description as 'the husband of Naomi'. She is no longer defined by her relationship to him, but vice versa. So the reader is instantly prepared for the shocking news of the early death of the apparent hero of the story.

The terse account gives no details about the death of Elimelech. But it leaves Naomi alone, with her two sons. For a decade, these three make their home in this foreign land, and in the course of that time, the two sons find wives – Moabite wives. It is worth recalling that such a practice is generally not encouraged in the early books of the Bible: sexual relations with Moabite women leads directly to a spiritual infidelity on the part of Israelite men in Numbers 25:1–3, and close community with Moabites is expressly forbidden to Israel in Deuteronomy 23:3–6. One wonders if there were no Israelite women, fellow sojourners in Moab, among whom Mahlon and Chilion might have sought wives.

The two Moabite women are Orpah and Ruth. We are given no insight into how they, or their families, felt about their marriages across the boundaries of race and culture. The etymology of their names seems less clear and so is presumably also less freighted. Ruth, it transpires later in the story (4:10), was the wife of Mahlon (and Orpah, therefore, was married to Chilion).

About a decade after the death of Elimelech, Naomi's two sons also died. Perhaps they died in the same incident; or perhaps their deaths were coincidental. Either way, the curtain comes down on this brief first scene in the drama, as Naomi is left alone with her daughters-in-law, 'without her two sons or her husband'. Naomi not only survived her husband (a tragic situation, especially in a patriarchal culture), but survived her children also – a personal disaster in any culture. She began the scene as a wife and a mother, but ends it as a childless widow. A story which began in crisis has, over the course of a decade, deteriorated into calamity. A migration which was intended to remedy poverty has brought destitution. There will surely have been many times during that period of at least a decade when Naomi questioned the wisdom of her decision-making: should she and Elimelech ever have left Bethlehem? Might she have returned to Bethlehem on the death of Elimelech? Should she have allowed her sons to marry Moabite women? What if…?

There is a reminder here that experiences of migration and displacement are often also experiences of bereavement – sometimes of multiple bereavements. It is worth dwelling on this introduction for a moment for the insight it offers into migrant lives. There are many Naomis in the world, stranded in a strange land, destitute, and desperate. Many treacherous journeys undertaken by contemporary migrants in search of a better life end in disaster. This story tells us nothing about Naomi's former life in Israel or her standing in Bethlehem, nor about the achievements of Elimelech at an earlier point in his life. This too is a common testimony among those who become migrants and asylum seekers: their former lives all too often count for nothing in their new country of residence and the stories of earlier chapters of their lives mostly go untold.

Nasir's Story

to Sheffield from Pakistan

Nasir's story is raw. His departure from his country of origin was relatively recent. As such, his testimony illustrates most vividly the migrant journey, from crisis and calamity, to migration and kinship, to subsistence and vulnerability. (Note also that names have been changed in this story to protect the identity of the people concerned.)

I grew up in Lahore, Pakistan. My family has been Christian as far back as I know. I am the youngest of my siblings, and all of us (in school and out of school) have experienced discrimination in small but persistent ways on account of our faith. The discrimination is more severe in employment, from colleagues and bosses: Christians are generally seen as fit only for menial jobs – when a Christian succeeds in securing an office job, for example, people will say, 'The cleaners are behind the desk now.'

After leaving school in 2009, I came to the UK to study for a degree in mechanical engineering at Doncaster College. I stayed until 2013 and returned home after that.

Our life circumstances changed in 2010 when my oldest brother, who had a successful business, was asked for help by a colleague and friend who wanted to convert to Christianity. Though my brother warned him of the trouble he would face, the man was determined, so he helped him. The result was that, first, that man himself had to flee (because his in-laws started to come after him), and then my brother had to flee. The man's family (together with some extremist people) blamed my brother for the man's conversion. The threats and attacks against him became increasingly violent, so he fled to the USA.

After my brother had gone, we assumed life would settle down again, but, in fact, occasional threats and harassment against my family continued, even after I returned to Pakistan in 2013. People would come to our house or confront us in the street to humiliate us or beat us or whatever.

I got married to Aman in 2020. My wife used to work for a Catholic charity that supported people facing harassment or persecution – such as having bogus blasphemy cases brought against them. Their work focused on villages and small towns because these attacks were frequent. My wife supported girls and young women who were especially vulnerable. After one particular case, she, too, became the focus of personal attacks. Even their efforts to make the school curriculum unified and less religiously biased were met with extreme opposition in the form of verbal and targeted threats on many occasions. For some months, we tried to escape the threats: moving house, even moving to a new city for a few months, hoping things would calm down. But repeatedly, people managed to track us down. Occasionally, someone would come to our house to 'talk' with my wife.

So, in mid-2023, we decided to leave. That was a hard decision. Our family is important to us, and we didn't want to leave them. We tried our best to survive, but eventually, our situation became untenable. We fled to the UK and as soon as we got to Heathrow, claimed asylum.

We were detained at the airport for four or five hours and interrogated. After processing, the Home Office transferred us to a hotel in Chelmsford. We arrived at the hotel around 2.00 am and were told that we would stay in the hotel until a decision was made on our asylum application. However, the next morning the hotel staff informed us about a letter from the Home Office requiring us to leave the hotel because we had about £1,500 with us, which we had declared at the airport. Because of this money we were not entitled to accommodation.

I offered to pay for us to stay there, but the hotel manager said his contract was exclusively with the Home Office, and so he could not accept paying guests – his hands were tied. When we tried to find alternatives, we couldn't – our passports had been held at the airport, so we had no identification papers, no bank cards, nothing.

Desperate, I contacted my oldest brother, a pastor in Virginia, USA. He is also a doctoral student at the University of Cambridge, at Wesley House. He contacted some people he knew here in the Methodist Church and explained our predicament, that we were a family with a small daughter, about to be made homeless, with nowhere to go.

Amazingly, the people at Cliff College, which is a Methodist college, offered us accommodation. A church in Chelmsford helped us with the transportation to Cliff College. We were stunned by the hospitality and welcome offered by the college staff and community. We have a one-bedroom flat, which is more than enough for us. We couldn't have asked for anything better.

Cliff College is in a small Derbyshire village, so the nearest big supermarket is a distance away; however, other college residents and church members generously drive us there when we need groceries. They make us feel like part of the community, invite us to events, etc. It's the same at All Saints' Church: the congregation has been fantastic. Being part of such a strong Christian community has been a great blessing.

We feel safe here and have become a part of the community. We have joined a local church where my wife and I serve actively. This community has become a second home to us. Our two-year-old daughter has made friends here. We stay in contact with our families in Pakistan via phone and social media. I did see my oldest brother when he came over from the USA in January: that was the first time I had seen him for 14 years!

As we wait for our asylum application to be processed, we are left in a state of uncertainty. The only communication we have received from the Home Office so far is our application registration (identity) cards.

With the backlog at the Home Office, it could take a long time for our asylum claims to be processed. The unknown future is a constant source of worry and stress for us.

Despite the challenges we have faced, we remain hopeful for a better future in the UK. We hope that our asylum application will be granted, allowing us to live without the constant threat of persecution. We are eager to contribute to the economy and wellbeing of this country, using our education, skills, and experience.

Study session one

To begin, read through the 'Guide to study materials' located at the end of the book (p. 135) to familiarise yourself with the format and intent of this material.

Participants are invited to prepare by reading pages 7–30.

For this session, you will need a candle and something with which to light it for the closing worship.

Welcome (15 minutes)

If group members do not already know one another well, it will be important to arrange a brief introduction, perhaps including name, home context, and church involvement.

Each group member is invited to say, in a sentence, what they hope they might get out of these six sessions.

Each group member is invited to respond to these questions:

- What's your favourite book or story?
- Do you have a favourite bit of the Bible?
- Do you have a migration/refugee story in your family? For how many generations has your family been settled in the country where you live?

The facilitator may like to lead an opening prayer, committing to God the discussion and reflection which follows.

Word (40 minutes)

Before reading the short Bible text, allow 20 minutes to reflect together on the following:

- Has your experience of family been mostly positive or difficult?
- How do family and nation contribute to your sense of identity?
- On page 9 you will find some United Nations definitions:
  - a migrant is a person 'who lives in a country other than their place of birth'.
  - a refugee is a person who 'owing to well-founded fear is unable or unwilling to avail themselves of the protection of the country of their nationality'.
  - an asylum seeker is a person 'whose claim for refuge has not been finally decided'.
- Do any of these definitions surprise you?
- Do these terms help or hinder you in seeing migrants, refugees, and asylum seekers as individuals, with histories and hopes, fears and dreams?

Read the short Bible text together: Ruth 1:1-5 (20 minutes).

- Which of the named characters in this passage do you relate to most easily and why?
- Do any of the named characters in this passage remind you of individuals you know or have met in your community and why?
- Was there material in the exposition which sparked a new thought?

Work (20 minutes)

Look again at Victor's story, which begins on page 14. In the opening description, a paradigm of the whole migrant journey is described, which moves from crisis and calamity, to migration and kinship, to subsistence and vulnerability, to security and wellbeing, to integration and inheritance, and finally to contribution and legacy. Look also at Nasir's testimony, on page 27.

- At what point in his story do you think Victor was most vulnerable?
- What support do you imagine would have been most valuable to him then?
- Victor refers to the support he received from ASSIST. What strikes you about the way he describes that support?
- Victor spent 14 years in the asylum system. Who or what do you think is responsible for that?
- What challenged you most about Nasir's testimony?
- Nasir was evicted from Home Office accommodation without any means to secure shelter. What duty of care should there be towards people in the asylum system?

Worship (5 minutes)

Light a candle and spend a few minutes in silent reflection together, thinking especially of those around the world who are beginning on their migrant journeys right now and who have been plunged against their wills into 'crisis and calamity'. After a few minutes, close the session with this prayer:

Almighty and merciful God,
whose Son became a refugee and had no place to call his own;
look with mercy on those who today are fleeing from danger,
homeless and hungry.
Bless those who work to bring them relief;
inspire generosity and compassion in all our hearts;
and guide the nations of the world towards that day when all will
    rejoice in your kingdom of justice and of peace;
through Jesus Christ our Lord.
Amen.

If you have capacity

Investigate online the presence of migrants, asylum seekers, and refugees in your own community. Does your research throw up any surprises?

ACT I

MIGRATION AND KINSHIP

NAOMI'S EMPTINESS
(RUTH 1:6–22)

The famine referred to in verse 1 was a dearth of food only. Now Naomi has suffered a famine of kin too: she has no husband, no sons and – here the silence of the text speaks volumes – no grandchildren either. She came to Moab with little, and after a decade, has nothing. As a childless widow in a foreign country, her options for survival were presumably few – among them, giving herself into slavery was surely one. But news from Bethlehem opens up a more attractive possibility: to return home.

This first narrative episode in the story falls into three scenes, which chart a journey from Moab to Bethlehem, through a succession of dialogues. Scene 1 (verses 6–7) briefly recounts the start of a journey, as Naomi departs from Moab, accompanied by both daughters-in-law. Scene 2 (verses 8–18) is set on the journey and includes the first two pieces of dialogue: initially with both daughters-in-law (verses 8–14) and then with Ruth only (verses 15–18). Scene 3 (verses 19–22) then completes the journey, as the two women achieve their destination. It includes a third dialogue (verses 19–21), between Naomi and the women of Bethlehem.

The key word in this episode is *šub* (return, go back). It is used twelve times in just 17 verses (6, 7, 8, 10, 11, 12, 15 [x2], 16, 21, 22 [x2]), mostly with reference to the journey Naomi is contemplating, back home to Israel, but also to the choice open to her daughters-in-law, to go back to their families – the choice made by Orpah. In the Hebrew scriptures, and especially to a post-exilic readership, this is a word with very positive connotations of restoration and the reversal of fortunes.

Scene 1 (verses 6–7): the start of a journey, the departure from Moab

> [6]Then she started to return with her daughters-in-law from the country of Moab, for she had heard in the country of Moab that the LORD had had consideration for his people and given them food. [7]So she set out from the place where she had been living, she and her two daughters-in-law, and they went on their way to go back to the land of Judah.
>
> RUTH 1:6–7

It's worth noting that the main character of this Act (as in the Prologue) is not Ruth but Naomi. It is 'she' (verse 6) who begins the return journey home to Bethlehem. She does so because in the country of Moab she had heard 'the LORD had had consideration for his people and given them food' (literally, bread). This is the first of 18 carefully distributed references to the LORD in the book of Ruth. It is one of only two such references which are not on the lips of characters in the story, but are narrated reports of God's action. The other is in the parallel final Act, in 4:13. The first reference to the LORD, then, alerts the audience to a God who cares for his people and provides for them.

How Naomi had heard this news, the text does not say. But migrant communities have always sought to remain in contact with home. This is, of course, infinitely easier in a digital age, but was evidently possible for Naomi too. Presumably there were comings and goings between Moab and Israel, even between Naomi's current location and Bethlehem. Where our translation states that 'the LORD had had consideration for his people', the Hebrew is *paqad*, meaning 'visited'. This is a key term in Exodus (e.g. 3:16). Similarly, when we are told in verse 7 that Naomi 'set out', the Hebrew verb is *yatsa*, another word used repeatedly in the story of the Exodus. Together, these words help to frame Naomi's journey as an attempt to escape oppression and to find freedom in the promised land. Her journey would, after all, literally require a crossing of the River Jordan.

Verse 7 also reiterates what is stated in verse 6, that at the outset of the journey, Naomi was not alone: her two daughters-in-law set out with her, both of them apparently fully intent on making the journey with her.

Scene 2, part 1 (verses 8–14): on the journey

The first dialogue: Naomi and her daughters-in-law

> [8]But Naomi said to her two daughters-in-law, 'Go back each of you to your mother's house. May the LORD deal kindly with you, as you have dealt with the dead and with me. [9]The LORD grant that you may find security, each of you in the house of your husband.' Then she kissed them, and they wept aloud. [10]They said to her, 'No, we will return with you to your people.' [11]But Naomi said, 'Turn back, my daughters, why will you go with me? Do I still have sons in my womb that they may become your husbands? [12]Turn back, my daughters, go your way, for I am too old to have a husband. Even if I thought there was hope for me, even if I should have a husband tonight and bear sons, [13]would you then wait until they were grown? Would you then refrain from marrying? No, my daughters, it has been far more bitter for me than for you, because the hand of the LORD has turned against me.' [14]Then they wept aloud again. Orpah kissed her mother-in-law, but Ruth clung to her.
>
> RUTH 1:8–14

Naomi urges her daughters-in-law to return home. This is a common-sense proposal, surely: after the deaths of their husbands, why would Orpah and Ruth choose to go with their mother-in-law to a country they do not know, in all the economic and social exigency of widowhood, when they could remain among family and friends in a place they know and can navigate confidently?

The first great speech in the book, in verses 8 and 9, leaves no doubt that Naomi's urgings are genuinely motivated by goodwill: she longs for their fulfilment and security and believes their prospects will be better in their native Moab, among their own kin, than in Bethlehem, where they have never set foot. She urges Orpah and Ruth to return, each to their 'mother's house'. This is a slightly surprising term. 'Father's house' might have been expected, as in Genesis 38:11, for example. Where the rarer term 'mother's house' is used (e.g. in Genesis 24:28 and Song of Songs 3:4 and 8:2) it appears associated with matrimony. That seems to be the case here too: the term reinforces Naomi's wish that each of her daughters-in-law, returning each to their mother's house, would ultimately find security, each in the house of a new husband.

In her speech, Naomi twice invokes the name of the LORD and in doing so builds on the theme of the LORD's goodness established by the narrator in verse 6. She prays that the LORD will deal kindly with them in their mother's house, showing them *hesed* (loving kindness) there as they have shown to her and to the deceased men of the family, and granting the security a new husband will provide. It is startling that Naomi assumes the covenant God of Israel can deliver this loving kindness and security not only in Israel and not even for Israelites, but even in Moab and for Moabites.

Naomi's kisses, and the tears she shares with her daughters-in-law, underline the genuineness of her wishes for them and her distress at the prospect of their parting, which is reciprocated. There is genuine mutual affection between mother-in-law and daughters-in-law. Indeed, her offer is initially rejected by both Orpah and Ruth, who state their intent of returning with Naomi to her people.

Thus far, this first dialogue conforms to a pattern familiar in the Middle East to this day: a generous offer is made by one party and politely declined by the other; it is repeated and perhaps expanded by the first party and is only then gratefully accepted. Sure enough, in verses 11–13, Naomi elaborates on her proposal, laying out in full (in a series of rhetorical questions and in one of the longer speeches in the book) her inability to provide for the two younger women: she has no further sons to whom they could be married, and even if she were to bear sons (an unlikely prospect, since she is 'too old to have a husband'), would they seriously wait until those infants were grown men? 'Go home', she tells them. Three times she refers to them affectionately as 'my daughters'; and for the third time, but now more darkly, Naomi refers to the LORD: 'the hand of the LORD has turned against me', she laments (verse 13). Naomi understands the LORD to be the author of distressing developments in life, not only fulfilling ones. Like Job (in Job 2:10), she aspires to receive the bad 'at the hand of God' and not only the good. Naomi fears that if they insist on maintaining their close association with her, her daughters-in-law will only share in her adversity. Naomi can't envisage a future in which the hand of the LORD is with her, not against her, and she fears for what that might mean for Ruth and Orpah if they do not turn back to Moab.

Readers and hearers rather expect, in verse 14, that with much weeping and kissing, the two daughters-in-law will now heed Naomi's urgings and will part company with her. And indeed, this is what happens – but only with Orpah. Orpah's is the sensible choice and in the narra-tive no blame attaches to her decision. Her mother-in-law has firmly instructed her, and her response can be seen as a reluctant deferral to that instruction. Indeed, Naomi promptly holds up Orpah's decision as exemplary, one that Ruth might yet follow.

By contrast, Ruth clings to her mother-in-law – the Hebrew word is the same as the one used in Genesis 2:24, where it is said that 'a man leaves his father and his mother and clings to his wife, and they become one flesh'. Ruth is already (in advance of her speech in verses 16–17) show-ing an extraordinary degree of family commitment to Naomi. Migration generally brings such commitments into sharp focus.

Scene 2, part 2 (verses 15–18): on the journey

The second dialogue: Naomi and Ruth

> [15]So she said, 'See, your sister-in-law has gone back to her people and to her gods; return after your sister-in-law.' [16]But Ruth said,
>
> 'Do not press me to leave you or to turn back from following you! Where you go, I will go; where you lodge, I will lodge; your people shall be my people, and your God my God. [17]Where you die, I will die – there will I be buried. May the LORD do thus and so to me, and more as well, if even death parts me from you!'
>
> [18]When Naomi saw that she was determined to go with her, she said no more to her.
>
> RUTH 1:15–18

Naomi speaks for the third time in verse 15, opening a second dialogue, this time with Ruth alone. She makes one last attempt to urge Ruth to follow Orpah's example. 'See!' she says, 'Your sister-in-law has gone back to her people and to her gods. Go with her.'

For all that Naomi has already indicated about her confidence that the LORD is able to bless Moabite people in Moab, she has also now revealed her acceptance that Moabite people generally worship Moabite gods, and that for Orpah, returning to her people inevitably meant returning to her gods. In this context, Ruth's pledge of allegiance in verses 16–17 is all the more surprising: she has not only embraced Naomi, but Naomi's God. This marks the climax of Ruth's fourfold commitment in verse 16: she binds herself to Naomi's journey, commits to the destination, embraces Naomi's people as her own, and ultimately claims Naomi's God as her own as well. She goes on in verse 17 to not only take Naomi's place of burial for her own (implying that her commitment to Naomi, her people, and her God will continue beyond the end of Naomi's life), but also call upon herself the LORD's most severe judgement if she should ever renege on this vow.

It is easy to gloss over the costliness of Ruth's commitment: it was a once-for-all decision, to turn her back on all that was familiar to her, quite possibly including other close family relationships and friendships, to go to a place she had (presumably) never been to before, where she would be a stranger with no obvious prospects or structures of support beyond her allegiance to Naomi and her trust in the LORD. It is the migrant's dilemma: to risk what is familiar, including what has been precious, in pursuit of something which might be better but is uncertain. Above all, this dilemma applies to relationships: almost every migrant leaves behind close family members; and almost every migrant forms new kin-relationships not shared by those who have been left behind.

Her speech surely demonstrates that Ruth has come to a lively trust in the LORD, despite being a Moabite (as the final verse of this chapter will forcibly remind us) and despite Naomi's own bitter experience of finding that the hand of the LORD has turned against her. This fierce determination eventually convinces Naomi, who gives up on the attempt to persuade Ruth to return home. Naomi's silence is not punitive. It is her gift to Ruth, signifying her acceptance of her daughter-in-law's decision.

Scene 3, part 1 (verses 19–21): the end of the journey – the arrival in Bethlehem

The third dialogue: the women of Bethlehem and Naomi

[19]So the two of them went on until they came to Bethlehem. When they came to Bethlehem, the whole town was stirred because of them; and the women said, 'Is this Naomi?' [20]She said to them,

'Call me no longer Naomi, call me Mara, for the Almighty has dealt bitterly with me. [21]I went away full, but the LORD has brought me back empty; why call me Naomi when the LORD has dealt harshly with me, and the Almighty has brought calamity upon me?'

RUTH 1:19–21

As in verses 1–5, the narrative passes over the challenges of the journey, but the trek from Moab to Bethlehem was surely even more danger-ous and arduous for Naomi and Ruth than the reverse journey had been for Naomi and her family a decade earlier. Back then she was younger, but crucially she was also in the company of an adult man and possibly also two young men. Migrant journeys are seldom easy or straightforward, but they are always most treacherous for women, especially unaccompanied women. We do not learn whether the two of them found company or travelled alone or whether there were crises along the way. But the fact that this story is set, as the very first verse tells us, 'in the days when the judges ruled' hardly encourages us to suppose their journey was safe.

Where the first two dialogues in this scene took place in Moab and were initiated by Naomi, the third takes place upon her arrival in Bethlehem and is initiated by the women of the city. (They will speak again, in chorus, in the partner 'Act' to this one, in 4:14–15 and 4:17.)

When Naomi and Ruth arrive at their destination, the whole town is stirred up on their account. The Hebrew word is ambiguous. It might mean the women were distressed, or equally, that they were excited. Probably a range of emotions is implied, causing them to cry out, 'Is this Naomi?' Since we know so little about the circumstances of Naomi's departure from Bethlehem all those years before (was she sent on her way with goodwill or recrimination?), we cannot know what this question conveyed, whether delight or resentment. Given that the women recognised their former neighbour, one can imagine the unspoken questions: 'Where is Elimelech? Where are Chilion and

Mahlon? Who is this with her?' Or perhaps the Moabite was as invisible to the women of Bethlehem as migrants often are to local people.

But the question provokes an outburst from Naomi, in which she rejects that identification: 'Call me no longer Naomi ('Lovely' or 'Sweetness')', she pleads. 'Call me Mara ('Bitter'), for the Almighty has dealt bitterly with me. I went away full, but the LORD has brought me back empty; why call me Naomi when the LORD has dealt harshly with me, and the Almighty has brought calamity upon me?'

'The Almighty, the LORD, the LORD, the Almighty' is a neat symmetrical pattern, but the sentiments are far from neat. Naomi attributes her harsh and bitter experience to the same LORD as the one to whom she was referring as the author of mercy and kindness earlier in chapter 1. Yet she speaks as a woman of faith: the LORD remains 'the LORD', and the Almighty remains 'Almighty' even when life has taken a turn Naomi would not have chosen and bitterly regrets. If, as the narrative rather assumes, this outpouring of grief was uttered within Ruth's hearing, it must have grieved her – given her utter commitment to Naomi – that her mother-in-law could describe her life as now empty. Or perhaps Ruth would have recognised this as the hyperbole of grief: if Naomi were truly full at the start of the story, she would presumably never have left Bethlehem. Naomi did, however, go away full of menfolk and has returned empty of them.

Contemporary western Christianity remains strangely unfamiliar and ill at ease with this deeply biblical tradition of protesting about – and even to – the LORD, the Almighty, on account of his action or inaction. From Job to Jeremiah, and often in the Psalms, Hebrew worshippers felt able to complain to God or about God as Naomi does here. It is a form of faithful prayer, not a falling away from it.

As a matter of fact, however, Naomi's request is not granted: the name Mara does not appear again in the book. Not only the narrator (frequently), but the workforce in Boaz's field (2:6), Boaz himself (4:5, 9), and even the women to whom Naomi is speaking directly here (4:17) all consistently continue to call her Naomi. Their continued use of her given name may be an affirmation that the LORD, the Almighty, might yet bless her with loveliness once more. Although she cannot see it, the others affirm that Naomi is not inevitably consigned to a life of bitterness.

Scene 3, part 2 (verse 22): the end of the journey – the arrival in Bethlehem

So Naomi returned together with Ruth the Moabite, her daughter-in-law, who came back with her from the country of Moab. They came to Bethlehem at the beginning of the barley harvest.

RUTH 1:22

This part of the story concludes with a summary statement: Naomi and Ruth have arrived safely in Bethlehem. Three things about the summary are noteworthy.

First, Ruth's origins (and with it, her migrant status) are emphasised, as they will be again just a few verses later, in 2:2 and 2:6.

Second, in language which underlines the extent to which she has bound herself with Naomi, she, as well as her mother-in-law, is described as having 'returned' and 'come back' to Bethlehem. In terms of the narrative, it is a fair assumption that in fact she had never been there before and was not actually returning. But such is her alliance to the returning Naomi that the word transfers naturally to her. Naomi's people are now, after all, her people. Migration has the effect of redefining kinship in this way.

Third, we are told they arrived 'at the beginning of the barley harvest'. This final phrase serves as a hint of good things to come: it encourages a hopeful anticipation in the audience for what might happen next.

Olena's Story

to Sheffield from Ukraine

Olena's story is still quite recent. Her departure from her country of origin took place only a few years ago. As such, her testimony illustrates vividly the migrant journey, from crisis and calamity, to migration and kinship, to subsistence and vulnerability, to security and wellbeing, and finally to contribution and legacy.

My name is Olena Taranukha. I am 49 years old. I am a Ukrainian, a successful woman, and the mother of three beautiful sons. I have a degree in economics. I used to work as an associate professor at the National Transport University in Kyiv, and was the co-owner of a business that provided people with transport services. I like to travel and learn more about other cultures. In my free time, I was engaged in music and painting. I am a Christian, a member of the Ukrainian Orthodox Church, and an integral part of my life is to attend Sunday worship and services on Feast Days, and to go on pilgrimage to holy places.

At the start of the full-scale Russian invasion of Ukraine on 24 February 2022, everything changed. I lost my job and my business and had to leave my apartment to flee with my children from the war with just our identity documents and two suitcases of belongings.

At first, I went to the deserted western part of Ukraine with my two younger sons and our cat. We lived in the Carpathian Mountains for some time and recovered a little from the shock and stress we had experienced. After two weeks, relatives from Cyprus invited us to their home, but we could not cross the border with the cat without the appropriate vaccinations and documents. We waited for my eldest son to return from abroad and left the cat with him and migrated to Cyprus.

Cyprus is a great destination for vacations, but we found we couldn't lead the active life we were used to. My children did not have the opportunity to study or attend sports clubs. We detected the weariness of our relatives from our stay in their small house. We could not stay there for long. So as soon as we learned about British aid for Ukrainian refugees, we began to look for a family that could provide us with housing and help. A family in Sheffield kindly welcomed us into their home – me and my two sons. But my parents, my aged grandmother, my brother, and my eldest son stayed in Ukraine.

Life in our new home became a kind of heaven on earth for my family. Our hosts became a second family for us and surrounded us with care and kindness. We felt as if we were in God's bosom. We found a safe place where we felt protected. In addition, the house had a stunningly beautiful garden, where we saw a family of foxes and many squirrels and birds. Thanks to the help of our hosts, my sons were able to continue their studies in local schools, to play football, and to box. Our hosts were always ready to come to our aid and helped us in solving life situations that often arose due to lack of knowledge of the language.

Their willingness to open the doors of their home, to welcome with a sincere heart and warm hospitality a family of strangers who were in need of help, was wonderful. In the past two years in England, I have benefitted from the experience of living in a multicultural environment: I have met tolerance, respect, and a friendly attitude towards people of different cultures, races, and religions.

Living in another country, however, is not a tourist trip and presents many challenges. Forced relocation, the loss of a place of residence and of familiar surroundings and habits of life, the limited ability to plan, and the complete uncertainty about the future traumatises the mind and negatively affects the psychological and emotional state. The loss of my job, business, position in society, and material goods made me think afresh about life. It has made me reassess my priorities and values. It may seem strange, but only thanks to the terrible war and the flight into the unknown with my children and only the most necessary belongings, have I felt like a free person, not burdened by material goods or status.

The most painful thing for me has been the impossibility of close communication with my relatives, and the lack of opportunity to go to church, to worship in my native language, or to pray with the people of my parish. Today, the biggest challenge for me is language. Without fluency in English, it is impossible to feel like a full-fledged member of society. I cannot find a job suited to my qualifications without fluency in the language and it takes time to learn a new language. The speed of language learning is complicated in my case by my age! In addition, even knowing the language in Britain, there are many accents that are difficult to distinguish and understand. The strange culture, with a different mentality, sometimes prevents us from understanding people correctly.

Also, after a year our accommodation with our hosts came to an end and we had to move into council accommodation. Especially in the first few weeks, and actually for the next seven months, as we were moved from temporary place to place, that was very hard. More recently we have moved into a permanent home and that is better.

The greatest desire of every Ukrainian is the end of the war. My most cherished wish is to meet on my native land with all my relatives under a peaceful sky. The war and years of living in England have changed and transformed my approaches to life. I have stopped planning and worrying about the future. I have started living simply and looking for joy in every day of my life, thanking God more for everything, appreciating every minute of life, giving love and support to people. I have learned to live in a changing environment, put away my ambitions, and understood simple things. The most important thing in life is the health of loved ones. You don't need much to live a happy life. It is enough to rejoice and be satisfied with what is, that everyone is alive and partially healthy. You need to give more, protect the feelings of others, hope for God's mercy, and trust him more.

Study session two

Participants are invited to prepare by reading pages 36–48.

For this session, you will need access to the text of Psalm 137 for the closing worship.

Welcome (15 minutes)

If the group has been joined by a new member, it will be important for everyone to introduce themselves again, perhaps including name, home situation, and church involvement.

Each group member is invited to respond to these questions:

- If you could spend tomorrow anywhere in the world, where would you go?
- What item of clothing that you currently own would you miss most?
- What is the most important thing that has happened to you in the past week?
- What has remained with you from last week's gathering?

The facilitator may like to lead an opening prayer, committing to God the discussion and reflection which follows.

Word (40 minutes)

Before reading the short Bible text, allow 20 minutes to reflect together:

- What has been your experience of moving house?
- Have you ever had to make a home in a new culture?

- If you have never moved very much or very far, what have been the biggest opportunities and challenges you have faced?
- If you have moved often or a long way, what have been the biggest opportunities and challenges you have faced?

Read the Bible text together: Ruth 1:6–22 (20 minutes).

Why not allocate four parts to members of the group: Narrator, Naomi, Ruth, and Orpah?

- Verses 6–7: Narrator; verses 8–9: Naomi; verse 10: Ruth and Orpah
- Verses 11–13: Naomi; verse 14: Narrator; verse 15: Naomi; verses 16–17: Ruth
- Verse 19: Narrator; verses 20–21: Naomi; verse 22: Narrator

- How you do you feel about the choice made by Orpah?
- How costly do you imagine it was for Ruth to make her choice?
- Was Naomi right to attribute her bitter experience to the LORD?
- Was there material in the exposition which sparked a new thought?

Work (20 minutes)

Read Olena's story. which begins on page 46. For over two years from February 2022, refugees fleeing the Russian invasion of Ukraine were granted a privileged status by the UK government, with automatic fast-tracked rights to citizenship and to work and to bring immediate family members over with them.

- Do you think this special provision was appropriate?
- Is it right that no such privileges are offered to refugees from other parts of the world where invasion is putting lives at risk, such as South Sudan or Gaza?
- Should the UK government generally seek to keep refugee families together?

Worship (5 minutes)

Psalm 137 is a song about the impossibility of singing a familiar song of ˙
worship to the Lord in a place of exile and oppression. It clearly dates
from the time when the people of Israel were captives in Babylon. The
last two verses are among the most shocking in the Bible.

Invite a member of the group to read the Psalm aloud, slowly. Others
are invited to note their emotions as the text is read and to offer these
feelings and thoughts to the Lord in silent prayer.

The group is invited to close by joining in this prayer together.

God of love and compassion: have mercy we pray
on the refugee family, seeking safety from violence;
on the migrant worker, bringing food to our tables;
on the asylum seekers, seeking justice for their families;
on the unaccompanied child, travelling in a dangerous world.

Give us hearts that break open
whenever our brothers and sisters turn to us.
Give us eyes to recognise a moment for grace instead of a threat.
Give us hands that reach out in welcome, but also in work,
for a world of justice until all homelands are safe and secure in
Jesus Christ our Lord.

If you have capacity

Could you write to your MP about the way migrants and refugees are
characterised in the media and in public debate?

ACT II

SUBSISTENCE AND VULNERABILITY

Ruth and Boaz in the field (Ruth 2)

O ne of the features which makes the book of Ruth such an appeal-
ing story is that almost every single character in it acts generously. There is really no one who acts meanly or selfishly. In Act I,
Naomi (though distressed and disheartened) nevertheless emerges
as a woman of stubborn faith, concerned not only for her own future
but for that of her two daughters-in-law. Ruth meanwhile manifests
a selfless loyalty and loving kindness. Orpah is no more criticised in
the text for the choice she makes than the next-of-kin will be in Act IV,
with whom Boaz will meet. The women of Bethlehem who lament with
Naomi at the end of Act I are likewise depicted sympathetically – as
are the other anonymous groups of people in the book: the labourers who work for Boaz in Act II and the elders of Bethlehem in Act IV.

If there were suspicions in Bethlehem about the newly arrived Moabite
taking up residence in their midst; if there was resentment at Naomi
for bringing this foreigner among them; if people harboured misgivings
about Ruth's intentions, the text does not acknowledge it. Instead,
early in Act II, we are introduced to Boaz. His experience of life has
been as full of prosperity as Naomi's has been of adversity. From the
outset he is introduced as a noble individual, and his behaviour in this
chapter justifies the description.

Act II forms a clear literary pairing with Act III. The former relates an initial encounter between Boaz and Ruth, which takes place by chance, by
day, outdoors and in public. The latter relates a subsequent encounter
between them, which takes place by design, by night, indoors and in
private. Act II falls into three parts: scene 1 (verses 1–3a) features Ruth
and Naomi at their home; scene 2 (verses 3b–16) features Ruth and
Boaz in the field; and scene 3 (verses 17–23) again features Ruth and

Naomi at their home. Act III will mirror this structure closely, with short scenes featuring Ruth and Naomi at home either side of a longer middle scene featuring Ruth and Boaz, only this time at the threshing-floor.

In Act II, the verb 'to glean' (*laqat*) unites the three scenes. The word comes no fewer than a dozen times in all, at least once in each scene (verses 2, 3, 7, 8, 15 [x2], 16, 17 [x2], 18, 19, 23). The middle scene offers us 'a day in the life of a gleaner', moving from early morning (verse 7) to lunchtime (verse 14) and to evening (verse 17). This longest scene includes three pieces of dialogue: the first is between Boaz and his workmen (verses 3–7); the second between Boaz and Ruth (verses 8–14); and the third (verses 15–16) between Boaz and his workmen once again.

Scene 1 (verses 1–3a): Ruth and Naomi at their home

> [1]Now Naomi had a kinsman on her husband's side, a prominent rich man, of the family of Elimelech, whose name was Boaz. [2]And Ruth the Moabite said to Naomi, 'Let me go to the field and glean among the ears of grain, behind someone in whose sight I may find favour.' She said to her, 'Go, my daughter.' [3]So she went.
>
> RUTH 2:1–3a

In Act I, notwithstanding Ruth's inspiring speech in verses 16–17, Naomi is undoubtedly the central character. This fact, together with certain slightly odd features in Act IV, has raised in the mind of some commentators the question whether this whole story might better be called the book of Naomi, rather than the book of Ruth. But in these opening verses of Act II, there is a decisive shift as Ruth begins to displace Naomi as the central figure – a shift indicated by the length of their respective speeches. Whereas the longer speeches in Act II belonged to Naomi, in verse 2 it is Ruth who speaks at greater length.

The naming of Naomi in verse 1 chiefly serves to introduce the reader to Boaz. Boaz is described first as kinsman to Naomi on her husband's side ('of the family of Elimelech') and second as 'a prominent rich man'. The Hebrew is *iš gibbôr chayil*: it might indeed mean he was a man of great wealth, but *iš gibbôr chayil* is a common expression in the Hebrew scriptures and is usually translated 'mighty man of valour', 'valiant warrior', or some equivalent (e.g. Joshua 6:2; 1 Samuel 9:1). It implies respect in the community and an element of courage or integrity, as well as power. Boaz was acknowledged to be a substantial person in Bethlehem – and reading verse 1 in isolation, the most natural reading is that he is being introduced as a possible levirate husband for Naomi. At any rate, the verse serves to heighten the expectation of the audience, to know how exactly this man will feature in the story.

The fact that Naomi herself has not taken any initiative to find food for herself and for Ruth, and has become reliant on her daughter-in-law, may suggest that she is languishing in hopelessness. It is as much as she can do to rouse herself to reply briefly (in just two words in the Hebrew) to Ruth's proposal.

Typically, forced migrants are most vulnerable immediately on arrival. Frequently, there is a period of day-to-day subsistence, when it is unclear where the next meal is coming from. This may not have been quite true for Ruth and Naomi – although a decade had passed, Naomi might well have been able to rely on historic support structures. The audience has the impression that she and Ruth are living in their own home, for example. But what follows also makes it plain that as yet they have no reliable source of food. It is to address this lack that Ruth now sets her mind.

Between Act I and Act II, all that separates two references to Ruth the Moabite is one verse (2:1). It is her designation in the final verse of chapter 1, and again in the second verse of chapter 2. The repetition is remarkable if the chapter break is ignored (chapter divisions as well as verse numbers were historically late additions to the text). It is very specifically as a Moabite, as a migrant, that Ruth speaks in this scene and takes action to provide for herself and for Naomi. In the spirit of Deuteronomy 24:19, she plans to go into the fields to glean. She would be doubly qualified to do so, as a widow and an alien, but she knows this might not be easy or be welcomed by the locals. She can only hope to find a field belonging to someone 'in whose sight I may find favour'.

'Needs must' is frequently the experience of newly settled forced migrants: no longer able to rely on inherited patterns of social and economic life, they may be driven to inhabit new roles and responsibilities. For some, this can be liberating: deprived of routines on which they previously depended, refugees can sometimes find themselves less dependent and more able to take new initiatives. A new situation, where old patterns no longer hold, may actually offer greater opportunity for agency, particularly for a female migrant. Perhaps Ruth experienced some exhilaration as she set out to provide for herself and for Naomi.

Scene 2, part 1 (verses 3b–7): Ruth and Boaz in the field

Boaz in dialogue with his men

She came and gleaned in the field behind the reapers. As it happened, she came to the part of the field belonging to Boaz, who was of the family of Elimelech. ⁴Just then Boaz came from Bethlehem. He said to the reapers, 'The LORD be with you.' They answered, 'The LORD bless you.' ⁵Then Boaz said to his servant who was in charge of the reapers, 'To whom does this young woman belong?' ⁶The servant who was in charge of the reapers answered, 'She is the Moabite who came back with Naomi from the country of Moab. ⁷She said, "Please let me glean and gather among the sheaves behind the reapers." So she came, and she has been on her feet from early this morning until now, without resting even for a moment.'

RUTH 2:3b–7

As Ruth sets out to provide, the Lord's providence intervenes as she duly finds herself in the field (or rather 'the part of the field') belonging to Boaz, whose relationship to Elimelech is repeated, lest the audience miss it. A literal translation of the Hebrew would be something like, 'As her luck lucked it, she came to the part of the field': there is a doubling of the vocabulary of fortune. If that were not already coincidence enough, 'just then' (we are supposed to marvel at the Lord's timing) Boaz himself arrives. The Hebrew is literally, '*Hinneh!* Behold! Boaz came from Bethlehem.' Ruth has not only chanced upon Boaz's field, she has done so at just the moment when the man himself appeared, so that she has the opportunity to meet him.

If our English translation had not already told us Boaz was a rich man, we could infer it from the fact that he owns not only fields, but also a retinue of men to work them. Having been told he is an *iš gibbôr chayil* (a man of great wealth), we now discover he is a man of faith. He greets his workers with the words, 'The LORD be with you', and they respond, 'The LORD bless you' (verse 4). Boaz is set before the audience as that rare human being: a rich man who may yet enter the kingdom of God, even though it is easier for a camel to pass through the eye of a needle.

Of course, Boaz's greeting and the reply of his men may be entirely conventional and religiously superficial, but it is worth noting that as an everyday greeting this exchange is recorded nowhere else in all of scripture. Rather, the impression that Boaz's words, and those of his workers, are the overspill of an authentic faith is strengthened by his obvious care for his labourers and their evident respect for him. Further, it emerges that Boaz is consistently alert to others: within moments of his arrival he has noticed the unfamiliar migrant among the gleaners. He knows both his workforce and his wider community well enough to spot the interloper. So Boaz asks after Ruth and his foreman tells him, 'She is the Moabite who came back with Naomi from Moab.' Here, Ruth's migrant status is laid bare: she is deprived of her name and only her ethnic origins are stated. But she is not just 'a Moabite': she is 'the Moabite' – apparently the story of her arrival is now well known in Bethlehem and apparently well regarded. Despite the foreman defining Ruth principally by her race, there is no further trace of xenophobia here, no animosity despite the ancient enmity between Israel and Moab. Rather, the foreman reports to Boaz, in a way that is generous and kind, both her polite request to be allowed to glean and her exceptionally hard work. Ruth may be a particularly diligent individual, but in fact the sheer struggle to survive almost always requires hard physical work (often menial work) for a migrant, especially in the early days.

Scene 2, part 2 (verses 8–14): Ruth and Boaz in the field

Boaz in dialogue with Ruth

8Then Boaz said to Ruth, 'Now listen, my daughter, do not go to glean in another field or leave this one, but keep close to my young women. 9Keep your eyes on the field that is being reaped, and follow behind them. I have ordered the young men not to bother you. If you get thirsty, go to the vessels and drink from what the young men have drawn.' 10Then she fell prostrate, with her face to the ground, and said to him, 'Why have I found favour in your sight, that you should take notice of me, when I am a foreigner?' 11But Boaz answered her, 'All that you have done for your mother-in-law since the death of your husband has been fully told me, and how you left your father and mother and your native land and came to a people that you did not know before. 12May the LORD reward you for your deeds, and may you have a full reward from the LORD, the God of Israel, under whose wings you have come for refuge!' 13Then she said, 'May I continue to find favour in your sight, my lord, for you have comforted me and spoken kindly to your servant, even though I am not one of your servants.'

> [14]At mealtime Boaz said to her, 'Come here, and eat some of this bread, and dip your morsel in the sour wine.' So she sat beside the reapers, and he heaped up for her some parched grain. She ate until she was satisfied, and she had some left over.
>
> RUTH 2:8–14

If there was room for doubt about the character of Boaz before now, his next step removes it as he proves himself sensitive to Ruth's vulnerability and extreme need. He strongly encourages her to commit herself to his estate, but his intentions in doing so are anything but predatory. There is a group of young women working alongside the male harvesters, sufficiently connected to Boaz for him to describe them as 'my young women'. He urges Ruth to associate herself with them.

For the first time since her arrival in Bethlehem, Ruth has the prospect of belonging to a group, of finding at least a hint of community. For female migrants it can be especially transformative to find female company and support. Nothing is said about the reception Ruth received among those other young women, whether it was warm or frosty, whether they reached out to embrace her or sought to keep their distance from her, but there is at least the hint of a prospect that among them Ruth will be able to take vital early steps towards healthy integration into Bethlehem's community. At any rate, the end of the chapter will tell us that Ruth 'stayed close to the young women of Boaz, gleaning to the end of the barley and wheat harvests' (verse 23) – and she was surely building up relationships with them over those weeks.

In verse 8 Boaz tells Ruth that (in a nice anticipation of modern 'anti-harassment' legislation in the workplace), he has ordered his young men not to pester her. The Hebrew word *naga* is usually translated 'touch' here, but it could equally be rendered 'strike', 'assault', or 'molest'. For all that Ruth has so far met nothing but generosity, there is a realism to Boaz to match Ruth's sober aspiration to 'find favour' with some field owner: a lack of racism is not to be taken for granted. Every young woman gleaning in the fields is vulnerable in proximity to the male workforce, but a migrant is all the more so. Ruth was, after all, taking gleanings that properly belonged to the destitute among Israelite women. Racism is often fiercest in times of scarcity, when outsiders are deemed to be taking what insiders believe is barely enough for them. Boaz has recognised this potential dynamic and has acted swiftly to afford Ruth some protection. If this kindness were not enough, he tells Ruth that she is welcome to have access to drinking water. Gleaning from dawn until midday in Israel in the season of the barley harvest is thirsty work. Normally in that culture, women drew water for men to drink and, in all likelihood, foreigners for Israelites; here Ruth is encouraged to drink from what the young men have drawn.

This generosity on the part of Boaz is so far beyond the call of duty that Ruth responds fervently. She falls at Boaz's feet and asks why she has found such favour, particularly given her migrant status. 'Why should you take notice of me', she asks, 'when I am a foreigner?' The Hebrew in verse 10 (*hakkirênî… nākrîyah*) is literally, 'You have known the unknown' or 'You have recognised the unrecognisable.'

Then comes the decisive speech in the Act and perhaps in the whole book. In verse 11, we discover that Boaz has been impressed by what he has heard about Ruth's loyalty to Naomi. He knows that Ruth has left her father and her mother and her native land and has come 'to a people that you did not know before'. Presumably it has become the talk of the town. Did the people of Bethlehem detect an echo of the story of Abraham, who also left his native land to go to a place and a people he did not know? 'May the LORD reward you for your deeds', he tells her, 'and may you have a full reward from the LORD, the God of Israel, under whose wings you come for refuge!' Boaz has faith in the God of Israel not only to respond to the needs of an individual, but also to repay goodness for goodness, to reward loyalty, and to provide refuge for all those who seek it under his wings – refuge not least for a Moabite migrant.

This extraordinary speech transforms Ruth's situation – or at least, it would appear that she took it to do so. She expresses the hope that she might continue to enjoy Boaz's favour (verse 13 is the third time in this Act we have met this word, after verses 2 and 10), expresses that she is comforted by his kind words, and describes herself as 'your servant, even though I am not one of your servants'. A relationship of sorts has been established by Boaz's kindness: she may still be a migrant, but she is no longer a stranger to him. She is 'your servant though not in fact your servant'. She and Naomi are not quite as destitute as before: the exceptional generosity manifested by Boaz has opened a possible route out of subsistence.

In keeping with her prior diligence, Ruth must then have returned to work because in verse 14, at the mealtime, Boaz has to call to her afresh. Previously he had given her permission to glean and had granted her access to water. Now, in a second act of kindness, he invites her to lunch. So Ruth finds herself sitting among the reapers, enjoying bread dipped in sour wine and even as much parched grain as she could eat until she was satisfied, with 'some left over'. For any refugee, the opportunity to eat in safe company represents a blissful development.

Scene 2, part 3 (verses 15–17): Ruth and Boaz in the field

Boaz in dialogue with Ruth

[15]When she got up to glean, Boaz instructed his young men, 'Let her glean even among the standing sheaves, and do not reproach her. [16]You must also pull out some handfuls for her from the bundles, and leave them for her to glean, and do not rebuke her.'

[17]So she gleaned in the field until evening. Then she beat out what she had gleaned, and it was about an ephah of barley.

RUTH 2:15–17

As the afternoon shift begins, Boaz initiates a third act of kindness – only this time Ruth was presumably entirely unaware of it, at least at the time. He instructs his workers to not rebuke her if she happens to stray from the edge of the field into the standing crop itself, but rather to contrive to ensure her 'gleanings' were enhanced: they are told to drop extra barley in Ruth's path. There was no obligation of Boaz to act in such a generous way. In permitting her to glean, Boaz demonstrated himself to be Torah-observant: he upheld the laws of the Pentateuch with regard to gleaning, laws which were precisely intended to provide for the widow, the orphan, and the alien. Now to his piety he adds remarkable liberality. Just as in verse 14 he heaped up parched grain for Ruth, here he continues to heap up his acts of kindness.

Ruth continued to glean until evening, and then worked on further, to beat out what she had gleaned: an ephah of barley.

Scene 3 (verses 18–23): Ruth and Naomi at their home

[18]She picked it up and came into the town, and her mother-in-law saw how much she had gleaned. Then she took out and gave her what was left over after she herself had been satisfied. [19]Her mother-in-law said to her, 'Where did you glean today? And where have you worked? Blessed be the man who took notice of you.' So she told her mother-in-law with whom she had worked, and said, 'The name of the man with whom I worked today is Boaz.' [20]Then Naomi said to her daughter-in-law, 'Blessed be he by the LORD, whose kindness has not forsaken the living or the dead!' Naomi also said to her, 'The man is a relative of ours, one of our nearest kin.' [21]Then Ruth the Moabite said, 'He even said to me, "Stay close by my servants, until they have finished all my harvest."' [22]Naomi said to Ruth, her daughter-in-law, 'It is better, my daughter, that you go out with his young women, otherwise you

> might be bothered in another field.' ²³So she stayed close to the young women of Boaz, gleaning until the end of the barley and wheat harvests; and she lived with her mother-in-law.
>
> RUTH 2:18–23

Ruth returns home to Naomi with her ephah of grain as well as the leftovers from her own lunch. Naomi (who has presumably been waiting anxiously for her daughter-in-law's return) is doubly astonished: first by the volume of what Ruth has gleaned and then by the cooked food.

Commentators are uncertain how much an ephah might have been, but Naomi's astonishment implies it was an unusually large amount for a single day's work. A reasonable estimate might be 15 kgs, where 1 kg would represent a good day's work. Even that smaller amount would be enough to feed Naomi and Ruth for several days. Naomi is unaware, at this point, where Ruth has been gleaning, but she knows that Ruth has surely been the beneficiary of exceptional generosity. When she asks Ruth where she ended up working, the Hebrew in her question is '*Ephoh*?', possibly a word play on ephah.

In her reply, at the end of verse 19, Ruth keeps Naomi in suspense for the longest possible time, leaving the name of her patron to the very last word (in Hebrew as in our English translation): 'The name of the man with whom I worked today is… Boaz.' Naomi's reaction is to break into praise of God: 'Blessed be he by the LORD,' she says, 'whose kindness [*hesed*] has not forgotten the living or the dead!' What has especially sparked her joy is the fact that, as she explains to Ruth, Boaz is a relative, 'one of our nearest kin'.

Clearly, Ruth's circumstances (and Naomi's) have taken a turn for the better. Indeed, there has been a transformation in Naomi: she is a more animated and hopeful figure at the end of scene 3 than she was at the start of scene 1.

Yet at two levels, despite some mitigation of their circumstances, Naomi and Ruth remain in a precarious situation.

First, there is a definite emphasis in these closing verses to Ruth's ongoing vulnerability as a migrant woman working in close proximity to young men. In relating to Naomi, in verse 21, what Boaz had told her, she slightly misrepresents him, whether knowingly or not. He had urged her (verse 8) to stay close to his young women. She tells Naomi he told her to 'stay close by my [male] servants', prompting Naomi rather anxiously to redirect her: 'It is better, my daughter,' she says in verse 22, 'that you go out with his young women, otherwise you might be bothered in another field.' The narrator then confirms that Ruth took heed of the warning and 'stayed close' to the young women of Boaz. In verse 23 and in verse 21, the Hebrew verb is 'to cling' – the very word used to describe Ruth's bond to Naomi in 1:14. Throughout, the potential threat to a young migrant woman working in close proximity to a group of local men is in view.

Second, although the text assures the reader in the final verse of the chapter that Ruth now enjoyed a short-term security, gleaning among the young women of Boaz until the end of the barley and wheat harvests, a period of perhaps two months, maybe three, this raises the question: 'What then?' What lies in store for Ruth and Naomi once the harvest season is over?

Hoda's story

TO MELBOURNE FROM IRAN

Hoda's story, like the two which follow, looks back on the initial migrant journey after the passage of more than a decade. So her story illustrates the trajectory from crisis and calamity, to migration and kinship, to subsistence and vulnerability, to security and wellbeing, to integration and inheritance, and finally to contribution and legacy.

My name is Hoda, and I am from Iran. I have been a part of the Emmanuel Anglican Church in Doncaster, Melbourne, Australia, since 2013, initially serving as a lay minister. In 2021, I was ordained as a priest in the Anglican diocese of Melbourne and currently serve as an associate priest at the church.

My decision to leave Iran was driven by the desire for a better life in peace and freedom, both for myself and my husband, Kaveh. In Iran, our families' differing traditions and expectations made it impossible for us to live together peacefully. I am from a very strict Muslim family; Kaveh's family was less religious. Additionally, Kaveh's family had a history of persecution by the Iranian regime, with his father being arrested multiple times and his grandfather being executed after the Iranian Revolution. The political pressures and restrictions in Iran, especially concerning Kaveh's newfound Christian faith, added to our reasons for seeking a new life elsewhere. But Kaveh's faith was very thin: mostly, it was part of his anti-government stance. He was a Christian because it was illegal to be! In any case, we left Iran two weeks after we were married, in early 2012.

Leaving Iran was a difficult decision, but we felt it was necessary for our wellbeing and future, though it meant leaving behind our families and everything we knew. However, we were driven by the hope of a better future for our growing family, free from the political pressures and restrictions we faced in Iran. The journey was not easy, but we were fortunate to have each other's support. We gathered our savings and fled to Indonesia, because it was one of two places (the other was Turkey) where we could go from Iran without a visa. But we were homeless there: we slept in the park for two nights. Our money was stolen. We had no food, and I was four months pregnant. One day, we had only ketchup to eat. But we met a Christian family, and their love was just different. They offered us hospitality; it was like a light in the darkness for us. They shared everything they had with us, so we wanted what they had.

One day, after many months, my husband started to pray, 'Lord, if you are there, help us to find a way out of this place.' Within a few days, we were put in contact with someone who promised to get us to Australia.

We ended up in Melbourne after a challenging journey by boat from Indonesia to Australia. First, we were taken on a small rowing boat to a larger vessel. The moment we saw it, we realised we had made a terrible mistake. There were no facilities on board. No food or water, and no sanitation. We were on the boat for 18 days and some days, we prayed to die. We could not imagine a good ending. But eventually, after 18 days, we ended up on an island which was an Australian dependency. There we were placed into the hands of the UN, and from there we were flown to Australia.

Arriving in Melbourne was a relief, and within three days after we arrived, we found a church – a welcoming community where we have been able to build a new life for ourselves and our children. I had suffered for many years from an emptiness in my heart. But then I went to the church for the first time, and I found real peace there. I also noticed how my husband had changed through his Christian faith. So I made a decision to be baptised.

The most positive part of my refugee experience has been finding peace and purpose through my faith in Jesus Christ. Despite challenges growing up in Iran, including my father's death and restrictions imposed by my brothers, I pursued education and independence. Leaving Iran with my husband, Kaveh, was a hard decision for a better life, but the way our journey to Australia led us to Christianity transformed our lives.

We are on temporary visas at present, and every three years we have to renew them. We are not allowed to access many government benefits, and this makes things difficult. Our visa status and the fear that some people have of 'boat people' can sometimes make us feel we are second-class citizens and not accepted here. We asylum seekers feel that we neither belong here nor to our country of birth; it is like feeling lost. It was hard that we were not eligible for free help from the government, so asylum seekers have to pay all study costs upfront. But most refugees are in a difficult financial situation, and they cannot afford to study. As English is not my first language, you have to overcome your fear of being judged or misunderstood. Then there are the financial struggles and the rejection – it takes courage to live here like this.

My hope and prayer is that Iranians find the true way and know Jesus as their Saviour rather than just as a prophet, to be set free from bondage and find true peace and a correct relationship with God through Jesus Christ. Also, the Farsi-speaking church has been severely damaged around the world due to a lack of awareness. Churches are young, and many people have been rejected from the church because of their attitude and thinking. We hope to welcome everyone and not insist on everyone thinking the same way about every issue. We want to be a church where it is okay to be yourself and to take your time listening, thinking, and finding your place. Our leadership is evident in the way we teach the faith, but we do nevertheless encourage questions, dialogue, and expressions of doubt.

Study session three

Participants are invited to prepare by reading pages 54–68.

For this session, you will need a collection of pebbles or stones, at least one for each member of the group for the closing worship.

Welcome (15 minutes)

From this point onwards in the course, it is assumed that members of the group no longer need to be introduced to one another. Of course, if this is not the case in your group, please take the time to make introductions.

Each group member is invited to respond to these questions:

- When you were a child, what sort of house did you live in?
- What's your favourite time of the day?
- What is the most important thing which has happened to you in the past week?
- What has remained with you from last week's gathering?

The facilitator may like to lead an opening prayer, committing to God the discussion and reflection which follows.

Word (40 minutes)

Before reading the Bible text, allow 15 minutes to reflect together:

- When have you depended most on the help of someone outside your family?

- Have you ever been unsure if you would find somewhere safe to spend the night?
- Have you ever had an experience of God's providence which seemed like sheer chance or good luck?

Read the Bible text together: Ruth 2 (20 minutes).

The chapter falls into three parts. Each part could be read by a different member of the group, to help you follow the flow of the story: voice one (verses 1–3a), voice two (verses 3b–17), and voice three (verses 18–23). Consider the below as you read:

- What strikes you most about the actions of Ruth in this episode?
- What strikes you most about the actions of Boaz in this episode?
- What does the speech of Boaz in verses 8–9 imply about the vulnerability of migrant workers and especially migrant women?
- Was there material in the exposition which sparked a new thought?

Work (20 minutes)

Read Hoda's story, which begins on page 66. She and Kaveh spent many months in acute vulnerability, without any guarantees of food or lodging. They subsisted very much from hand to mouth.

- Contrasting the experiences they had in Indonesia and Australia, what expectations do you think a refugee can reasonably have of the government to provide food and shelter?
- Hoda refers to people having a 'fear' of refugees arriving by boat? Where do you think this fear comes from? What role does the media play in contributing to this fear?
- For Hoda, the hospitality of Christians has been life-transforming. How does your church express its hospitality to outsiders?
- Does your local congregation engage with refugees and asylum seekers in a way that makes you proud to be a follower of Jesus?

Worship (5 minutes)

The facilitator may like to distribute a stone or pebble to each member of the group. Participants are invited to feel the size and shape and weight of the stone. You may like to ponder how it has been formed, how it has ended up in your hands today. Now let the stone represent an individual refugee or asylum seeker. This could be a person you know or one of the anonymous individuals arriving in Britain every week across the Channel in small boats. Consider the kind of journey they will surely have endured, like the one Hoda describes. Consider their unique creation by God, as unique as the stone in your hand.

You may like to bring the session to a close with this prayer:

Most merciful God,
we pray for the protection of refugees today and especially of the
*   vulnerable.*
Shield them from exploitation and abuse.
We hold before you pregnant women and new mothers,
the most elderly and frail,
and children who have been separated from their families or who
*   have been orphaned.*
Deliver them, we pray, into a place of safety,
where food and shelter are secure
and where those who might harm them can no longer reach them.
We ask this in the name of Jesus our Lord.
Amen.

If you have capacity

Sign up to a regular email from one of the charities campaigning for a better asylum system.

ACT III

SECURITY AND WELLBEING

Ruth and Boaz on the threshing-floor (Ruth 3)

A ct III of the book of Ruth forms a clear literary pairing with Act II. That Act relates an initial encounter between Boaz and Ruth, which takes place by chance, by day, outdoors and in public (where their conversation was likely overheard), as a result of which some mitigation of their vulnerability and subsistence is achieved for Ruth and Naomi. The sequel in this act relates a subsequent encounter between them, which takes place by design, by night, indoors and in private (where their conversation was probably not overheard), as a result of which more permanent security and wellbeing is achieved (or at least promised) for Ruth and Naomi. Just as Act II fell into three parts, with short scenes featuring Ruth and Naomi at home, either side of a longer middle scene featuring Ruth and Boaz, so does Act III.

There are further parallels between Acts II and III, in the respective central sections: in both cases Boaz enquires about Ruth's identity (2:5; 3:9), in both he deems her actions praiseworthy (2:11–12; 3:10), and in both he provides her with food (2:14; 3:15). There is a further parallel in the final scene of the two acts: in both, in her report of her encounter with Boaz, Ruth relates to Naomi something he said to her which was not recorded in the middle scene (2:21; 3:17).

It follows that Naomi is in the background of the present act just as she was in Act II. She is 'on stage' at home in the first five verses and reappears at the end of the scene for the final three verses, but she is absent for the majority of the action, in verses 6–15. Yet she is the one who directs matters 'behind the scenes'. The renewed vigour which she exuded in scene 3 of Act II is further evident here. In the opening verses, she outlines for Ruth an audacious scheme – a scheme full of risk, but which (if successful) would secure their long-term future.

She counsels a young foreign female field-worker to proposition an older Israelite male land-owner. In that context, it is significant that this is the only act in the book in which Ruth's ethnic origins are not emphasised. When her name does appear, in verse 9, on her own lips, it is without the descriptor 'the Moabite'.

Scene 1 (verses 1–5): Ruth and Naomi at their home

¹Naomi her mother-in-law said to her, 'My daughter, I need to seek some security for you, so that it may be well with you. ²Now here is our kinsman Boaz, with whose young women you have been working. See, he is winnowing barley tonight at the threshing-floor. ³Now wash and anoint yourself, and put on your best clothes and go down to the threshing-floor; but do not make yourself known to the man until he has finished eating and drinking. ⁴When he lies down, observe the place where he lies; then, go and uncover his feet and lie down; and he will tell you what to do.' ⁵She said to her, 'All that you tell me I will do.'

RUTH 3:1–5

In verses 1–4, Naomi utters one of the longer speeches in the book. She speaks 55 words in Hebrew to the handful of words with which Ruth responds in verse 5. Her opening sentence is an echo of the very first words she utters in this book, 'The LORD grant that you may find security' (1:9), only now she says, asserting her own agency, 'My daughter, I need to seek some security for you, so that it may be well with you'. Ruth has reached that point in a migrant's journey, or at least Naomi discerns that she has, when it is timely to look beyond subsistence.

In what follows, Naomi lays out for Ruth an intrepid plan. She has presumably been pondering the precariousness of their situation and the uncertainty of their future beyond the end of the harvest season.

She has discerned the possibility of a truly long-term means of security and her speech urges Ruth to seize the moment. What she proposes is bold, to say the least. Her ruse might fall short of an outright seduction, but the erotic overtones are plain, and she is certainly encouraging Ruth to proposition Boaz.

Step by step, in considerable detail, Naomi instructs her daughter-in-law. First, Ruth is to wash, to wear perfume, and to put on her best clothes. She is to go to the threshing-floor in search of Boaz, looking and smelling her best. Then Ruth is to wait, before approaching Boaz, until he has finished eating and drinking and has lain down. Until then, she is to conceal herself. Finally, marking carefully the place where Boaz is sleeping, Ruth is to approach him, to uncover his feet, and to lie down with him.

Clearly, Naomi is counselling Ruth to initiate an intimacy with Boaz which in that culture properly belonged to marriage and would have been regarded as deeply inappropriate outside it. A proposal of marriage is in effect to be made by a woman to a man, by the younger to the older, by a migrant to a native citizen. For that reason, even if Ruth did manage to observe with care where Boaz lay down, it was a plan fraught with risk – as others have observed, the plan is risqué as well as risky. As a result, there were real potential negative implications if the plan went wrong, for Naomi as well as for Ruth.

Scene 2, part 1 (verses 6–13): Ruth and Boaz at the threshing-floor – in the night

[6]So she went down to the threshing-floor and did just as her mother-in-law had instructed her. [7]When Boaz had eaten and drunk, and he was in a contented mood, he went to lie down at the end of the heap of grain. Then she came stealthily and uncovered his feet and lay down. [8]At midnight the man was startled

and turned over, and there, lying at his feet, was a woman! [9]He said, 'Who are you?' And she answered, 'I am Ruth, your servant; spread your cloak over your servant, for you are next-of-kin.' [10]He said, 'May you be blessed by the LORD, my daughter; this last instance of your loyalty is better than the first; you have not gone after young men, whether poor or rich. [11]And now, my daughter, do not be afraid; I will do for you all that you ask, for all the assembly of my people know that you are a worthy woman. [12]But now, though it is true that I am a near kinsman, there is another kinsman more closely related than I. [13]Remain this night, and in the morning, if he will act as next-of-kin for you, good; let him do so. If he is not willing to act as next-of-kin for you, then, as the LORD lives, I will act as next-of-kin for you. Lie down until the morning.'

RUTH 3:6–13

Ruth does as she is told. She waits until Boaz has had plenty to eat and drink and has gone to lie down 'in a contented mood'. Then, stealthily, she 'uncovers his feet' and lies down with him. It is possible that the word 'feet' is a euphemism for genitals here and in verse 4 – as it certainly is in Isaiah 7:20, Judges 3:24, 1 Samuel 24:3, and probably is also in Exodus 4:25. However, the phrase 'lying at his feet' in the very next verse and in verse 14 perhaps encourages the literal sense here. Nevertheless, the intimacy implied in the act of uncovering any part of a man's body, even quite literally just his feet, in the dark, when he is asleep, is a potential scandal.

Some commentators attempt to minimise the sexual connotations of what is described. It is true that there is an element of sexual restraint in the episode: no intercourse between Boaz and Ruth is recorded in Act III, and Act IV appears to suggest that their sexual relationship was only consummated after she became his wife (4:13). Moreover, in terms of the narrative, it is hard to see how Boaz could genuinely have sought to do the right thing by the man who had the prior rights as kinsman-redeemer if he had pre-empted the situation by having sex with Ruth.

Nevertheless, Ruth's need for stealth indicates how improper and potentially disgraceful she knew her behaviour to be. Her actions are all the more suggestive for being so carefully clandestine. She tiptoes at the edge of taboo: the conclusion of her actions will be that a man and a woman, not married to one another, are lying together in the dark, in secret, one of them at least partly disrobed, the other looking and smelling as attractive as possible. Boaz recognised the impropriety too. Why else, at end of the scene, was he concerned (verse 14) that 'it must not be known that the woman came to the threshing-floor' – let alone a migrant woman, an outsider who might seem to be supplanting sexually the young women with whom she has been working through the harvest season? It was vital to Boaz's public reputation that Ruth should leave as surreptitiously as she had arrived, precisely because her actions could so easily create offence.

So when Boaz awakes about midnight, no wonder the text says he is startled. 'Who are you?' he asks. It's not obvious to him what woman would be so reckless as to make her way on to the threshing-floor, let alone to place herself in such a compromising position with him. 'Ruth,' she says. 'Spread your coat over your servant, for you are next-of-kin.'

In verse 6, we were told that Ruth 'did just as her mother-in-law had instructed her', and it is true that Ruth's actions in verse 7 follow closely the instructions Naomi had given her in verse 4. But at this point, Ruth is improvising creatively. Where Naomi had advised Ruth 'he will tell you what to do' (verse 4), here Ruth is in effect telling Boaz what she wishes him to do.

Acknowleding Boaz as next-of-kin and her doing exactly as her mother-in-law had instructed make it clear that Ruth isn't seeking a casual sexual encounter, but a relationship of protection. Where our English translation states, 'Spread your cloak over your servant', the Hebrew is more literally, 'Take your servant under your wing.' The same language is used in Ezekiel 16:8, and there the association with marriage is explicit, if metaphorical. The LORD says to Israel through the prophet: 'I spread the edge of my cloak [wing] over you, and covered your nakedness:

I pledged myself to you and entered into a covenant with you, says the Lord GOD, and you became mine.' What Ruth is soliciting is a covenant commitment from Boaz. In fact, she echoes here the language Boaz himself had used in 2:12, when he expressed the hope that she would have a full reward for her deeds from the LORD, the God of Israel, under whose wings 'you have come for refuge'. In effect, Ruth is inviting Boaz to be the answer to his own prayer. Similarly, when Ruth refers to Boaz as 'next-of-kin' she is inviting him to accept responsibility for her long-term wellbeing and security. Precisely what the obligations of a gō'ēl (kinsman-redeemer) in ancient Israel were (and specifically, whether they included levirate marriage of the sort outlined in e.g. Deuteronomy 25:5–10) is unclear. But Naomi (2:20), Ruth (here in 3:9), and Boaz himself (3:12–13) all appear to assume they at least provided a legitimate basis for marriage.

At this point in the narrative there were presumably choices open to Boaz. What was to prevent him, after all, from taking advantage of the situation for his own sexual gratification? The power differential between him and the woman is extreme. Equally, he might have been appalled by her manoeuvre, raising the alarm and shaming Ruth publicly, cursing her and dismissing her as a harlot.

In fact, Boaz chooses to accept the implied proposal of marriage. In his response, he refers twice to the LORD. The references correspond to the two ways in which Boaz demonstrates his integrity in this moment. First, he takes no advantage of Ruth. She has made herself extremely vulnerable. It's dark. He's eaten and drunk well. It's the middle of the night. There are no obvious witnesses and, in any case, he is the most powerful person on the threshing-floor. What will he do now? Wonderfully, his immediate instinct is to think not of himself; his concern is rather for Ruth and for her welfare and blessing. 'The LORD bless you,' he says. He sees her actions as born not of opportunism but of loyalty and kindness (hesed). 'You could have run after younger men,' he says, 'but out of regard for your mother-in-law and your late husband's family, you have sought out a kinsman. You had already established a reputation in Bethlehem as a worthy woman; now you've proved it again.' Boaz describes Ruth as a woman of noble character. The Hebrew is *eshet chayil* – the exact words which introduce the poem in praise of 'a virtuous wife' in Proverbs 31:10. The description corresponds to that of Boaz himself in 2:1 as an *iš gibbôr chayil*, a man of great standing. In their nobility of character, Ruth and Boaz are a match for each other.

But there's a twist in the tale. How Ruth's heart must have lifted when Boaz told her, 'Do not be afraid; I will do for you all that you ask.' And how her heart must have sunk again when he at once goes on to report that Naomi has an even closer kinsman than himself, with a prior claim to act as a redeemer. Did Ruth and Naomi not know about this other man?

Here is the second illustration of Boaz's integrity. He commits himself to acting honourably towards that other man, as well as towards Ruth: 'If he will act as next-of-kin for you, good; let him do so. If he is not willing to act as next-of-kin for you, then, as the LORD lives, I will act as next-of-kin for you.' Perhaps, though, this was not entirely unwelcome news to Ruth: one way or another, whether by Boaz or by this other man, she now knows that she will (as Naomi had prayed for her at the outset of the story in 1:9) 'find security… in the house of [a] husband'.

Finally, Boaz invites Ruth to sleep beside him until the morning. That option would certainly have been safer for Ruth than for her to make her way home to Naomi at midnight. How much sleep will have been possible for either Ruth or Boaz is moot: the minds of both will doubtless have been racing in anticipation of how matters might work out.

Scene 2, part 2 (verses 14–15): Ruth and Boaz at the threshing-floor – in the morning

[14]So she lay at his feet until morning, but got up before one person could recognise another; for he said, 'It must not be known that the woman came to the threshing-floor.' [15]Then he said, 'Bring

> the cloak you are wearing and hold it out.' So she held it, and
> he measured out six measures of barley, and put it on her back;
> then he went into the city.
>
> RUTH 3:14–15

Perhaps the food and wine Boaz had consumed earlier enabled him
to fall asleep more readily than Ruth. At any rate, she rose first, 'before
one person could recognise another', so that the scandal of a woman's
presence at the threshing-floor would not be known. The longer Ruth
remained beside Boaz, the greater the risk that she would be discovered.
Such a development could, at the very least, have impacted unhelpfully on the negotiation he intended to open with the nearer kinsman.

In verse 14, Ruth is anonymously 'the woman'; that reference is more
than balanced by the anonymised references to Boaz as 'the man' in
verses 3, 8, 16, and 18. It is as if the narrator is colluding with the couple
in keeping their assignation as discreet as can be.

Boaz had chosen to lie 'at the end of the heap of grain' (verse 7). So it was
convenient, as they both prepared to leave, for him to load a bountiful
(if indefinite) supply – 'six scoops' – of barley into her shawl, if not as
a dowry at least as a token of his commitment. The text assumes that
Ruth then departed for home, but its focus remains on Boaz, who left
at once for the city, presumably to settle matters as soon as possible.

Scene 3 (verses 16–18): Ruth and Naomi at their home

> [16]She came to her mother-in-law, who said, 'How did things
> go with you, my daughter?' Then she told her all that the man
> had done for her, [17]saying, 'He gave me these six measures of
> barley, for he said, "Do not go back to your mother-in-law empty-
> handed."' [18]She replied, 'Wait, my daughter, until you learn how

> the matter turns out, for the man will not rest, but will settle the
> matter today.'
> RUTH 3:16–18

Naomi (who has presumably also endured a sleepless night) was waiting to find out how her plan has turned out. Although she asks directly,
'How did things go with you, my daughter?', presumably the sight of the
substantial supply of grain on Ruth's back was already an indication of
the answer. When Ruth explains in full what had happened and what
Boaz had promised to do, she reports a piece of conversation which
is new. In loading up Ruth with those six measures of grain, Boaz had
apparently said: 'Do not go back to your mother-in-law empty-handed.'
The consideration Boaz shows towards Naomi, over and above his
consideration for Ruth, is impressive.

Ruth's brief speech in verse 17 is her last in the book. It is appropriate
that they are words of loyal affection for her mother-in-law. Indeed, it
is possible to see this short and final speech as a gentle belated riposte
by Ruth to Naomi's lament in 1:20–21: certainly the same Hebrew
word for 'empty' (*reqam*) is used on both places. Naomi is on the way
to renewed fullness.

Naomi's reply (likewise her final utterance in the book) is encouraging.
She confidently assures Ruth that there won't be a long wait: Boaz will
sort things out without delay. That too is a lovely character reference for
Boaz. Naomi knows what he is like and is certain he will keep his word.

Boaz emerges in this chapter as a man whose trust in God's faithfulness
has shaped him in faithfulness too. His behaviour in private, in Act III, is
at one with his behaviour in public, in Act II. And his behaviour towards
Naomi and Ruth is at one with his behaviour towards his unnamed
male relative. That is integrity.

Moe Win's story

TO MELBOURNE FROM MYANMAR

Moe Win's story, like the one before it and the one which follows, looks back on the initial migrant journey after the passage of more than a decade. So his story illustrates the trajectory from crisis and calamity, migration and kinship, to subsistence and vulnerability, to security and wellbeing, to integration and inheritance, and finally to contribution and legacy .

I belong to the Karen ethnic group in Myanmar (formerly called Burma), the second largest ethnic group in Myanmar but a group which has been oppressed by the military dictatorship. There is a religious aspect to the persecution: many Karen people (like my mother) are Christian, while some (like my father) are Buddhist. I grew up in a Karen village close to the border with Thailand. In 1991, the military took over our village and drove us all out and across the border to a refugee camp in Thailand, called Mae La. To this day, it is not possible for us to go back.

At that time, there were 50,000–60,000 refugees in that camp. It was like a prison, with a fence. We had no freedom to come and go in Thailand, because we had no papers. If you went out of the prison, you risked being deported back to Burma. That happened to me once: I went outside the camp and was arrested and taken back to Burma – and then it was very hard for me to get back into the refugee camp.

I was nine years old when I first arrived in the camp and I was there for 14 years, with my parents and my three younger sisters and one younger brother. All my teenage years were spent inside that place. I completed my education inside the camp and was even trained to be a teacher – but it was at about that time that I was invited to apply to become a refugee to Australia.

I began to go to Sunday school in the camp and that is where I began to learn what it means to be a Christian. My faith became important to me, and I began to exercise some leadership, in the Sunday school and with the youth. One experience was especially formative: one day about a year before I came to Australia, when I was about 21 years old, I slipped and fell 20 feet down a shaft into a cave. I remember thinking, 'I am going to die,' and praying, 'O God, please keep me alive – I will do anything you ask me to do with my life.' It took my uncle and some family members three hours to pull me out of there.

One of our Karen community leaders who had been living in Australia came back to the refugee camp and encouraged others of us to apply through the United Nations High Commissioner for Refugees. At that time Australia was quite open to receiving refugees. The process of application for refugee status took about a year. We applied in 2002 and in 2005 we received permission to go to Australia: my parents, my younger sisters, and me. But we left my younger brother, cousins, and other relatives in the camp. Later they also came. Many Karen refugees preferred to apply to go to America because the process was quicker.

From the refugee camp we took a bus to the airport at Bangkok, in the care of the United Nations International Organization for Migration. We chose to fly to Melbourne, because there was already a strong Karen community here. The Karen community in Melbourne is now very big. Even in the city of Wyndham, the suburb where I now live, there are over 4,000 Karen people. But the flow of new arrivals is slower now: this year there have been maybe only three new families. That's not because the need for refuge from the camp has fallen; it's because the Australian government policy towards refugees has changed.

When we first arrived, we stayed with a friend – all six of us. But after a few months, we got a house. Then a new family arrived and for a while, they came to live with us. It has been like that from 2005, for the past 20 years: we help each other.

When I first arrived, I did a language school – I had only a few words of English before that. I was not confident to speak English so I had to start from the beginning. But I had a keen interest in film and media, and making movies and I pursued that as a hobby. I began looking for work.

Meanwhile, I found a church of Karen people – though at that time we were worshipping in a house. We did that for maybe three years. Each week, we would take it in turns to lead the worship. We felt we needed to worship in our own language – partly because many of our community don't really understand English. But gradually the community began to recognise it needed its own priest and encouraged me to explore ordination. I remembered my promise to God back in the camp, but I felt unworthy (especially because of my lack of education), so I ran away from that sense of calling and did not continue a discernment process. But after two years, I looked again at the needs of the Karen people and I came back to a discernment process. I prayed: 'O God, I am scared, but if you help me I will do this.' I did some training here in Melbourne, and the college was very helpful in supporting me to improve my English.

I was ordained in 2018. I am now married, with a son. My wife was in another refugee camp in Thailand – not the same one where I grew up. I met her when I went back to visit. When we were first married, she remained in Thailand. Our first child was born while my wife was still there. Three times, our application for her to come to Australia was refused. Then came Covid. But about four years ago, she and my son joined me here in Melbourne, and now we have a second child, born here. Now we are raising our family here and the future is full of hope.

STUDY SESSION FOUR

Participants are invited to prepare by reading pages 74–85.

For the closing worship at the end of this session, you will need a globe or a map of the world, as large as possible.

Welcome (15 minutes)

Each group member is invited to respond to these questions:

- What would you miss if you had to do without electricity for a week?
- What is the best thing for you about this time of the year?
- What is the most important thing which has happened to you in the past week?
- What has remained with you from last week's gathering?

The facilitator may like to lead an opening prayer, committing to God the discussion and reflection which follows.

Word (40 minutes)

Before reading the short Bible text, allow 20 minutes to reflect together:

- What most contributes to your feeling of security or insecurity?
- What most enhances or undermines your sense of wellbeing?
- How do different people relate to each other in your country? Consider differences such as age, gender, race, and class. To what extent are these ways of relating to each other helpful or unhelpful for society/community?

Read the Bible text together: Ruth 3 (20 minutes).

Ruth 3 is a clear 'pair' with Ruth 2, which we read last week. So why not read it in the same way, with each of the three parts being read by a different member of the group, to help you follow the flow of the story: voice one (verses 1–5), voice two (verses 6–15), and voice three (verses 16–18).

- What strikes you most about the scheme proposed by Naomi in verses 1–4?
- What strikes you most about the actions of Ruth in this episode?
- What strikes you most about the actions of Boaz in this episode?
- Do you think of Ruth as powerful or powerless at this point in the story?
- Was there material in the exposition which sparked a new thought?

Work (20 minutes)

Read Moe Win's story, which begins on page 83. Moe Win basically grew up in a refugee camp: he was a young boy of nine when he arrived and a grown man of 23 by the time he left.

- Do you think of him as powerful or powerless at this point in the story?
- What contributed to and what limited his security and wellbeing in the camp?
- What contributes to and what limits his security and wellbeing in Melbourne?
- Moe Win now leads a Karen-speaking congregation in Melbourne. Why do you think it is important for refugees and asylum seekers to worship in their native tongue?
- In Australia, he took English classes. How important do you think it is for refugees and asylum seekers to learn the local language?
- Moe Win relates how the Australian government has changed its policy to become more closed to refugees. How should

governments balance an unchanging moral obligation with shifting practical and economic considerations?

Worship (5 minutes)

Take a few minutes exploring the globe/world map. Can you find all the places from which the migrants in *Come for Refuge* originated: Zimbabwe, Pakistan, Ukraine, Iran, Myanmar (Burma), South Sudan, and Chile? Have you met, or are you aware of, asylum seekers and refugees arriving in your country from other places. Can you find those places too?

Spend a moment commending to God the world he has made, in all its brokenness and with all its displaced people. You may like to close the session by saying this prayer:

Lord Jesus,
you yourself had to flee for refuge and no refugee is a stranger
*   to you.*
We pray today for refugees on the move:
for those travelling to refugee camps, forced to relocate either
*   within their country or in their country of asylum.*
Heal the hearts of those who have endured the greatest trauma.
We pray for our community and for our church,
that both may be places of sanctuary and healing, security and
*   wellbeing for those in distress,*
to the glory of your name.
Amen.

If you have capacity

Some media outlets consistently paint a negative picture of migrants and refugees. They also generally rely on advertising revenue. Could you consider your purchasing decisions in this context?

ACT IV

INTEGRATION AND INHERITANCE

Naomi's fullness (Ruth 4:1–17)

Act IV serves as a parallel to Act I. These are the only two scenes in which the narrative acknowledges a direct intervention by the LORD (at the beginning of Act I, 1:6; and at the end of Act IV, 4:13), in both cases to grant fertility, first to the fields of Bethlehem and then to the womb of Ruth. These are also the only two scenes in which the women of Bethlehem appear as a chorus (1:19 and 4:14–15). In some respects, the figure of Orpah in Act I has her parallel in the unnamed kinsman-redeemer in Act IV: both initially commit to a course of action which promises to be significant for the story, but then undergo a change of mind which results in their disappearance from the narrative.

One of the unusual features of the book of Ruth is the extent to which the story emphasises the agency and conveys the perspectives of its female characters, and indeed of Naomi (1:6–15; 1:20–22; 3:1–5; 3:16–18; 4:14–17) as much as of Ruth (1:16–19; 2:2–23). This feature is at its most noteworthy in the final scene (4:13–17) of this fourth act of the drama, in which the voice of the women is offered almost directly as a counterweight to that of the male elders of Bethlehem, when they celebrate the child to whom Ruth has given birth as a boy born to Naomi.

However, this act also includes the only part of the story (in verses 1–12) told entirely from the male perspective and in which the presence and activity of women is completely absent. Although both women are named (Naomi in verse 9 and Ruth in verse 10), there is no recognition in these verses of the role they have played in engineering the developments described, nor of the benefits which will follow for them as a result of what transpires.

The act divides into three scenes: scene 1 (verses 1–8), Boaz in conversation with an anonymous next-of-kin at the city gate; scene 2 (verses 9–12), Boaz in conversation with the elders and all the people – still at the city gate; scene 3 (verses 13–17), the spotlight returns to Naomi (rather than Ruth), who is the recipient of a joyful affirmation by the women of the city.

Scene 1 (verses 1–8): at the city gate – Boaz in conversation with the next-of-kin

[1]No sooner had Boaz gone up to the gate and sat down there than the next-of-kin, of whom Boaz had spoken, came passing by. So Boaz said, 'Come over, friend; sit down here.' And he went over and sat down. [2]Then Boaz took ten men of the elders of the city, and said, 'Sit down here'; so they sat down. [3]He then said to the next-of-kin, 'Naomi, who has come back from the country of Moab, is selling the parcel of land that belonged to our kinsman Elimelech. [4]So I thought I would tell you of it, and say: Buy it in the presence of those sitting here, and in the presence of the elders of my people. If you will redeem it, redeem it; but if you will not, tell me, so that I may know; for there is no one prior to you to redeem it, and I come after you.' So he said, 'I will redeem it.' [5]Then Boaz said, 'The day you acquire the field from the hand of Naomi, you are also acquiring Ruth the Moabite, the widow of the dead man, to maintain the dead man's name on his inheritance.' [6]At this, the next-of-kin said, 'I cannot redeem it for myself without damaging my own inheritance. Take my right of redemption yourself, for I cannot redeem it.'

[7]Now this was the custom in former times in Israel concerning redeeming and exchanging: to confirm a transaction, one party took off a sandal and gave it to the other; this was the manner of attesting in Israel. [8]So when the next-of-kin said to Boaz, 'Acquire it for yourself', he took off his sandal.

RUTH 4:1–8

Boaz is as good as his word, uttered in 3:13. He makes his way to the city gate and sits down. Then 'behold!' (*hinnêh*), the very next-of-kin to whom Boaz had been referring in the previous act comes walking by, just as Boaz himself had happened along in Act II, right when Ruth had begun her gleaning. The exclamation *hinnêh* in the Hebrew scriptures is often an invitation to the reader to 'behold' the providence of God at work. Boaz calls out to his relative, invites him over, and sits him down formally. He then summons ten elders of the community (a quorum, presumably, like the *minyan* required in most Jewish circles before public prayer can take place).

The urgency and purposefulness of Boaz's actions is conveyed by the repetition of his name, four times in just the opening two verses. In the Hebrew text, the first of these instances is (a little unusually) the very first word of the chapter (as Naomi's had been in Act II). By contrast, the nearer next-of-kin remains unnamed. The Hebrew translated 'friend' in verse 1, when the man is addressed by Boaz, is *peloni almoni*, perhaps better rendered 'thingamajig', 'whatshisname', or 'so-and-so'. The term may be slightly pejorative. In a narrative, and indeed an act, in which names are so significant (see, not least, verses 5, 10, 11, 14, 17), this man's anonymity is a deliberate ploy to render him invisible to the audience.

This first scene is dominated by the vocabulary of redemption. The Hebrew word *gō'êl*, which occurs four times in this scene (verses 1, 3, 6, 8, as well as 2:20 and 3:13) is notoriously difficult to translate, though 'kinsman-redeemer' is a frequent choice. The NRSV has opted for 'next-of-kin', but with a footnote to indicate that a more literal sense would be 'one with the right to redeem'. The disadvantage of putting 'next-of-kin', of course, is that it fails to maintain the emphasis in these verses on redemption. In addition to those four references to *gō'êl*, similar words (including *geullah*, redemption) are to be found another seven times in this scene (verses 4 [x4], 6 [x2], 7 [x1]).

Aspects of the narrative are puzzling at this point, without a doubt. The text raises many questions. Our understanding of the conventions and obligations around redemption in ancient Israel is very limited. Clearly, the transaction at the heart of this scene assumes that more than one adult male in a family clan might be deemed to be a *gōʾēl* – and indeed, the first time we meet this word in the story, on the lips of Naomi in 2:20, it is a plural: she describes Boaz to Ruth as 'one of our kinsman-redeemers'. But precisely how one qualified to be a *gōʾēl* and who might be excluded, how priority was established and how far individual discretion could be exercised – much of this information is lost to us.

Moreover, the news disclosed by Boaz in his opening words, to the effect that Naomi has a parcel of land to sell also comes as a surprise to the audience, since the narrative has presented her until now as utterly destitute and 'empty'. One possibility is that Elimelech had sacrificed the leasehold of this parcel of land when he left for Moab, or at some point before that, but had retained the freehold, and that it is ownership of the freehold which is being debated at this point. The freehold would be of no immediate benefit to Naomi, but might have future value to Boaz or the other man. Alternatively, it might be that Naomi is seeking help to 'redeem' the leasehold. But it is also unclear how the language of redemption relates to the language of buying, selling, and acquiring: the terms appear to be used interchangeably in verses 3–10.

It is also unclear how the rights and responsibilities of a *gōʾēl* with regard to the acquiring of land relates to the rights of responsibilities of a *gōʾēl* with regard to acquiring a widow and her daughter-in-law. The connection was apparently obvious to Boaz in verses 9–10, but seems at first to have evaded the other kinsman-redeemer! Again, quite how Boaz has come to know about this parcel of land at this point, when the nearer next-of-kin is apparently oblivious to it, we are not told. Finally, it is also unclear why the obligation to acquire Ruth and Naomi was a fatal obstacle to the other man in his aspiration to redeem Elimelech's land, when it was not so for Boaz. Presumably their family situation was significantly different, but we do not know in what respects.

These puzzles expose how little we know about the way in which inheritance laws operated in ancient Israel. Yet for all the uncertainties, the basic parameters of the discussion between Boaz and his relative remain intelligible. Boaz sets out the position in verse 3: 'Naomi is selling some land. You're the one primarily entitled to buy it; but if you don't, I will, since I am next in line of entitlement after you.' To this, the kinsman replies that he would indeed like to redeem the land and this provokes Boaz to spell out the implications: 'If you acquire the land', he explains, 'you inevitably acquire Naomi and Ruth too.' Ruth is confusingly described as 'the widow of the dead man', and once again her ethnic origins and refugee status are stressed: she is Ruth the Moabite.

This may be the most significant of all the occasions in this story when Ruth's ethnic origins are underlined. It is explicit in the text that acquiring Naomi and Ruth would somehow damage the man's own inheritance, and for this reason he publicly relinquishes his right to them and to Elimelech's land, clearing the path for Boaz. But the speed and finality with which the potential gō'ēl changes his mind directly after the reference to Ruth's migrant status suggests that this was for him at least part of the obstacle.

At this point, the kinsman removes his sandal and passes it to Boaz. This action is sufficiently odd to require an explanation in verse 7: 'Now this was the custom in former times in Israel concerning redeeming and exchanging: to confirm a transaction, the one took off a sandal and gave it to the other. This was the manner of attesting in Israel.'

Most commentators rightly observe about this sentence that the editorial note about what used to happen 'in former times' in Israel is clear evidence that the final form of the book of Ruth dates from a period well after the one in which it is set. What is less often observed is how close this gesture is to one described in Deuteronomy 25:7–10 – and yet also how far from it. The juxtaposition of the two texts is striking. The passage in Deuteronomy explores a scenario analogous but not identical to the one in Act IV: when a man 'has no desire to marry his brother's widow'. It sets out the steps which might be taken to persuade him to do the honourable thing. But if he continues to refuse, then (in front of the elders of the town at the gate), 'his brother's wife shall pull off his sandal and spit in his face'. That man's family, the passage concludes, will henceforward be known as 'the house of him whose sandal was pulled off'.

For all the apparent overlap between that passage and this scene (elders, gate, levirate marriage, and a sandal), there are also obvious differences: Ruth and Naomi are apparently absent, the elders make no attempt to challenge the man's decision, he himself removes his own sandal rather than having it pulled off by a woman, there is no hint that in declining to act as *gō'ēl* he was acting shamefully, and there is no spitting. In our story, the man apparently retains his honour in the community.

Scene 2 (verses 9–12): at the city gate – Boaz in conversation with the elders and all the people

[9]Then Boaz said to the elders and all the people, 'Today you are witnesses that I have acquired from the hand of Naomi all that belonged to Elimelech and all that belonged to Chilion and Mahlon. [10]I have also acquired Ruth the Moabite, the wife of Mahlon, to be my wife, to maintain the dead man's name on his inheritance, in order that the name of the dead may not be cut off from his kindred and from the gate of his native place; today you are witnesses.' [11]Then all the people who were at the gate, along with the elders, said, 'We are witnesses. May the LORD make the woman who is coming into your house like Rachel and Leah, who together built up the house of Israel. May you produce children in Ephrathah and bestow a name in Bethlehem; [12]and, through the children that the LORD will give you by this young woman, may your house be like the house of Perez, whom Tamar bore to Judah.'

RUTH 4:9–12

Boaz accepts the proffered sandal, and the transaction is complete: all that had once belonged to Elimelech, and also to Mahlon and to Chilion, now passes to him 'from the hand of Naomi'. The text specifies in verse 10 that it was, however, Ruth (the Moabite) who became Boaz's wife and not Naomi – presumably only because Naomi was (as her speech had made clear at the outset of the story, in 1:11) beyond the age of child-bearing. The union of Boaz with Ruth is the central focus of a neat chiasm in verses 9 and 10:

> today you are witnesses,
>   Elimelech, Mahlon and Chilion,
>   Ruth the Moabite… to be my wife,
>   the dead man, the name of the dead,
> today you are witnesses.

It is also only in verse 10 that the reader discovers to which of Naomi's two sons Ruth was married. Act I never specified that it was Mahlon.

Boaz had addressed his speech to 'the elders and all the people'. His words prompted an outpouring of joy and well-wishing from 'all the people at the gate, along with the elders'. The switch in order may not be inconsequential. The point is that the redemption effected in scene 1 is not a purely private matter, not a cause of rejoicing only to Boaz, Naomi, and Ruth as the individuals directly involved. The redemption is a celebration not only for them, nor also only for the elders, but for all the people. Boaz stated as much: the outcome of what Boaz has done is that Elimelech (and with him, Mahlon and Chilion) would 'not be cut off from his kindred and from the gate of his native place'.

Four things about the exclamation of the people are worth noting.

First, Ruth is oddly anonymous here not once but twice. She is 'the woman who is coming into your house' in verse 11 and 'this young woman' in verse 12. This anonymisation is best viewed as a preparation for the honouring of Naomi by the women of Bethlehem in the final scene. The fact that it is not an attempt to marginalise Ruth, or to denigrate her on account of her migrant status is demonstrated by two things. One is that she has already in this act been designated 'the Moabite' (both times by her new husband, in verse 5 and verse 10). The other, perhaps more startlingly, thing is that it is the wish of all the people for Ruth to be nothing less than a new 'Rachel and Leah, who together built up the house of Israel'. These were the principal wives of Jacob/Israel, who with their maids (Bilhah and Zilpah) bore the twelve sons who in turn fathered the twelve tribes of Israel. It is hard to see what the people might have wished for Ruth in this moment which could have conveyed more fully their affirmation and inclusion of her, and her complete integration into the community at Bethlehem, than to liken her to those two great matriarchs of Israel.

Second, the people wish that the children Ruth will give to Boaz (or rather that the LORD will give to Boaz through Ruth) will make his house 'like the house of Perez, whom Tamar bore to Judah'. The reference to Tamar is significant. Her story, told in Genesis 38, has multiple points of contact with Ruth's story – although the differences are also great. She was almost certainly a Canaanite, widowed (several times) after marriage into an Israelite family. In order to secure her rights, Tamar disguised herself as a prostitute and seduced her father-in-law, Judah. She was, then, another non-Israelite who through some version of levirate marriage, achieved acceptance and inclusion in Israel.

Third, at the heart of the prayer of all the people for Boaz is the wish that he might continue to grow in nobility and valour. The NRSV rather obscures this by rendering the end of verse 11 as: 'May you produce children in Ephrathah and bestow a name in Bethlehem.' It is, of course, true that the desire for progeny is an almost universal one in human experience, but perhaps especially in agrarian cultures and among migrant communities. That desire has particular urgency in the context of this story, in which childlessness is precisely the problem that the narrative sets out to resolve (1:1–4, 11–13) and the reference to off-spring (literally, 'seed' – in effect a pun in the context of this narrative) is certainly there in the Hebrew text in verse 12. However, the final line in verse 11 simply says: 'May you *chayil* in Ephrathah and have a name in Bethlehem.' The word *chayil* we have met before, in 2:1 and in 3:11. Here it might be best translated: 'May you prosper.' Children might be implied, but the closer association is with noble character and valour.

Fourth, and finally, 'all the people' become the latest characters in the narrative to invoke the name of the LORD (verses 11–12). In so doing they join Naomi and Ruth, Boaz, and his workmen. They will be followed in this respect in the next scene by the women of Bethlehem. The name of the LORD comes easily to the lips of the people of this community. They confess him as the one who alone bestows the blessing of an inheritance.

Scene 3 (verses 13–17): a son is born to Naomi

> [13]So Boaz took Ruth and she became his wife. When they came together, the LORD made her conceive, and she bore a son. [14] Then the women said to Naomi, 'Blessed be the LORD, who has not left you this day without next-of-kin; and may his name be renowned in Israel! [15]He shall be to you a restorer of life and a nourisher of your old age; for your daughter-in-law who loves you, who is more to you than seven sons, has borne him.' [16]Then Naomi took the child and laid him in her bosom, and became his nurse. [17]The women of the neighbourhood gave him a name, saying, 'A son has been born to Naomi.' They named him Obed; he became the father of Jesse, the father of David.
>
> RUTH 4:13–17

In verse 13, the story achieves its happy ending. Boaz takes Ruth in marriage and 'she became his wife'. The narrative charts a definite progression in Ruth's relationship to Boaz. She initially described herself as a foreigner to him (2:10), then as his servant girl (*shiphchah*), 'even though I am not one of [his] servants' (2:13), then as his servant (*amah*, 3:9). Finally, she is his wife.

The LORD duly made Ruth conceive (after the apparent barrenness of her ten-year-long previous marriage) and she bore a son to Boaz. As it happens, this is only the second action attributed directly to the LORD in the book after the provision of bread in Bethlehem, related in 1:6 (in the companion act to this one). There is a difference, however: in 1:6 the LORD's action is something which has happened in a distant land and is only being reported to Naomi and Ruth; here, they are the direct beneficiaries of the LORD's work. This is also only the second reference to the LORD by the narrator, compared with 16 references on the lips of characters in the drama. The last of these references comes in verse 14, when the women of the community celebrate with Naomi, with a final blessing of the LORD, who has not left her without a next-of-kin.

The name of Ruth occurs for the final time in the story in verse 13. It is pleasing, somehow, that the name stands alone, without the descriptor 'the Moabite'. This lack of the descriptor was also characteristic of the first such namings (1:4, 14, 16), all situated in Moab. She first becomes Ruth the Moabite in 1:22, on arrival in Bethlehem, and is so named another four times (2:2, 21; 4:5, 10). After 1:22, she is only plain Ruth at 2:8, 2:22, 3:9, and 4:13. The final reference about her comes in verse 15, when the women celebrate her love for Naomi, and describe Ruth as meaning 'more to you than seven sons'. In a patriarchal culture, this would be an extraordinary acclamation of any daughter-in-law; it is all the more remarkable given that it is spoken of a Moabite. Ruth's extraordinary loyalty to Naomi, so profoundly expressed in the parallel Act I of the story, was not acknowledged at that time, but it is now given due recognition.

The focus on Naomi in verses 14–17 is unmistakeable and a little surprising. After they are named in verse 13, both Ruth and Boaz are in effect sidelined. But in this way, the narrative brings the calamity of chapter 1 (which was primarily Naomi's calamity) to a tidy conclusion.

In particular, these verses correspond to 1:19–21, when the women of the city asked, 'Is this Naomi?', only for the widow to reply, 'Call me no longer Naomi, call me Mara.' The repeated naming of Naomi in these verses reverses that plea. Now she is no longer Mara (bitter) but Naomi (pleasant) once more.

It is, therefore, with Naomi that the women of Bethlehem rejoice, in verses 14 and 15, at the prospect that the newborn child will be 'a restorer of life' to her and (in a rather wonderful phrase) 'a nourisher of [her] old age'. It is Naomi who cuddles the baby in verse 16 and cares for him. (The Hebrew *ōmenet* merely means 'nurse' in the broadest sense. There is no necessary implication of breastfeeding.) And it is as Naomi's son that the baby is named by the women of Bethlehem in verse 17. This is the only occasion in the entire Hebrew scriptures when a child is given a name by anyone other than a parent. Perhaps it serves as a further mark of how fully the offspring of Boaz and Ruth the Moabite has been accepted into the community.

The final sentence of verse 17 is, of course, the sting in the tale: this infant is not just any old baby. Obed turns out to be the father of Jesse and the grandfather of King David. So in the providence of God, the migrant Ruth turns out to be the great-grandmother of Israel's greatest king. What a legacy the Moabite refugee bequeaths not only to the people of Bethlehem, who received her with loving kindness, but also to all Israel. Conversely, what a glorious future might have been lost to Israel if the people of Bethlehem had responded with hostility to the migrant in their midst. It is not always necessary to wait four generations to see the rich contribution refugees can make to the communities which receive them, but equally that richness is not necessarily immediately obvious.

By the end of Act IV, Ruth enjoys both integration in Bethlehem and an inheritance in Israel.

David's story

to Melbourne from South Sudan

David's story, like the two which precede it, looks back on the initial migrant journey after the passage of more than a decade. So his story illustrates the trajectory from crisis and calamity, to migration and kinship, to subsistence and vulnerability, to security and wellbeing, to integration and inheritance, and finally to contribution and legacy.

My name is David, and I'm from South Sudan – which was part of Sudan until 2011, when it became a separate nation-state. I grew up on a farm in a village, and that's where I was when the civil war started. I was 14 years old. At that time I was already a Christian; I was taught the catechism. There were no priests; it was left to lay leaders to teach the gospel. We used to wait for priests to come to baptise us.

When the war began, my village was on the border. It was one of the first to be destroyed completely. I was left with nothing, except to become a soldier. I went to Ethiopia to train as a soldier. I fought for ten years and became a major in the army. I was shot four times. The last time, I had a bullet in my eye and lost some sight, so I was discharged from the army.

At that point I was sent to neighbouring Kenya for treatment. I had got married, and I went with my wife to a refugee camp, and with a child. I have never been back to South Sudan – the ongoing war made it impossible. This was 1995. I spent ten years in that camp. There were 850,000 refugees there from all over the continent. In fact, we called it 'Little Africa'.

Then, after ten years, and now with two children, I had a summons from the United Nations High Commissioner for Refugees. I had to submit documents, and I was accepted for interview, with my family, and the lawyer was very impressed with my application. I was granted permanent residence in Australia.

But the process took eight months, and during that time my wife gave birth to another child. When the visa came through, it was for a couple and two children only, not three. I had four weeks to make a decision: to stay in the camp with my newborn daughter or to go to Australia with my wife and older children. I was lucky enough to have my mother-in-law with us in the camp. She said: 'I have a decision for you. Is your wife good? Do you like her character? If so, I will bring your daughter up the same way.' So we left, with our two older children. But later I was able to negotiate with the immigration office and after another eight months, our daughter came too.

The best part since we arrived in Australia has been the education. I now have eight children, and the schools have been wonderful. My children are progressing well. This education was never possible for me in Sudan. And we have felt welcomed by the Anglican Church. The church answered a lot of our questions. I have got a job working in an abattoir.

The biggest challenge has been the cultural context. When we first arrived, my wife had no English, because she had never gone to school. We arrived from a completely remote area into the civilised world: the world of electricity, the world of the internet. When we were brought to our accommodation on our first day, we did not know what to do. We looked for a place to build a fire for cooking; we did not recognise the oven. We had to go to the supermarket, and when we went, we looked around: we recognised bread, some meat maybe, some fruit maybe. In the bathroom, we discovered the water was hot and cold. We could control the temperature! That was completely new for us: in Sudan and in Kenya we never had the choice of how hot or cold we wanted our bath to be; the temperature of the water was decided by nature.

So for my wife and for me it was a great challenge to adapt to the new situation. But our children became 'Australian' very quickly. That was difficult. It has been even more difficult as they have become teenagers. There are a lot of challenges in this area. In Africa, the extended family would bring up the children, but not here. Five of our children have been born in Australia and have no experience of Sudan.

The future is very bright. Our kids are growing up as African-Australians. We hope they will retain some African values (like community) as well as enjoying the freedom and opportunity of Australia.

Study session five

Participants are invited to prepare by reading pages 90–103.

No additional resources are necessary for this session – but the facilitator might like to experiment with the hand gestures suggested to accompany the Lord's Prayer in the closing worship.

Welcome (15 minutes)

Each group member is invited to respond to these questions:

- What is the most important thing which has happened to you in the past week?
- What has remained with you from last week's gathering?
- If your house was on fire, and every living thing was safe, what one object (or set of things) would you rescue?
- If you were given £250,000, how would you use it?

The facilitator may like to lead an opening prayer, committing to God the discussion and reflection to come.

Word (40 minutes)

Before reading the short Bible text, allow 20 minutes to reflect together:

- What are the most important communities to which you belong?
- What binds those communities together?
- Have you ever felt like an outsider, excluded from a community?
- What helps you to belong?

Read the Bible text together: Ruth 4:1–17 (20 minutes).

This passage is the 'twin' of Ruth 1:6–22, so you might like to read it in the same way that you read those verses, by having different people read the lines of: the narrator (most of verse 1, verse 7, verse 13, verse 16); Boaz (the end of verse 1, most of verses 2–5, verses 9–10); the next-of-kin (a bit of verse 4, verse 6, verse 8), the people at the gate (verses 11–12); and the women (verse 14, verse 17).

- What are the signs that Ruth now belongs in Bethlehem?
- Is this a story about Ruth's integration and inheritance or Naomi's?
- What difference do the members of the community make in this episode?
- Was there material in the exposition which sparked a new thought?

Work (20 minutes)

Read David's story, which begins on page 101. Like Moe Win last week, David spent many years in a refugee camp.

- To what extent do you think he experienced belonging and community in the refugee camp in Kenya?
- To what extent does he testify to finding belonging and community in Melbourne?
- What do you make of the way David describes the integration of his children into Australian culture: how do you assess the gains and losses of the next generation?
- When westerners move overseas for a better life, we tend to call them 'ex-pats' rather than migrants. Why do you suppose that is?
- If you sought refuge in another country, how well do you think you could embrace a new language, new customs, and maybe even a new way to dress?
- How can a local congregation help migrants and refugees to find belonging and community?

Worship (5 minutes)

For Christians, our sense of community and belonging depends ultimately on the coming kingdom of God. So this week, our session closes with the slow recital of the Lord's Prayer, with accompanying hand gestures. This… works… best… done… very… slowly…

Our Father in heaven (*hands above the head, index finger pointing up*)

Hallowed be your name (*hands above the head, thumbs up*)

Your kingdom come (*hands on the head, fingers up, as a crown*)

Your will be done (*fist planted on the palm of the other hand*)

On earth as in heaven (*hands make the shape of a circle or ball*)

Give us today our daily bread (*hands outstretched palms upwards*)

And forgive us our sins (*arms folded in an X across the chest*)

As we forgive those who sin against us (*one hand down, one held against the heart*)

And lead us not into temptation (*hand pointing directly ahead*)

But deliver us from evil	(*hands as fists, forearms crossed in front*)
For the kingdom	(*one hand as fist, raised triumphantly*)
The power and the glory are yours	(*repeat above*)
Now and forever. Amen.	(*hands folded in usual praying position to end*)

If you have capacity

Could you volunteer for a local charity working with asylum seekers and refugees?

EPILOGUE

CONTRIBUTION AND LEGACY

The renewal of a family line (Ruth 4:18–22)

A first genealogy, from which Ruth's name is absent

> ¹⁸Now these are the descendants of Perez: Perez became the father of Hezron, ¹⁹Hezron of Ram, Ram of Amminadab, ²⁰Amminadab of Nahshon, Nahshon of Salmon, ²¹Salmon of Boaz, Boaz of Obed, ²²Obed of Jesse, and Jesse of David.
>
> RUTH 4:18–22

If the prologue (Ruth 1:1–4) was a catalogue of untimely deaths which together threatened the end of a family line, the answering epilogue chronicles the survival of that family line. Together with the prologue, the epilogue is the only part in the book which lacks a reference to the LORD.

The concluding verses of the book of Ruth set the births of Obed, Jesse, and David into genealogical context. It is presumably the prior reference to Perez in 4:12 (itself presumably triggered by the likeness of Tamar's story to Ruth's), which accounts for the fact that the genealogy begins with his name, rather than with Judah's or even Jacob's. Had the list begun with Jacob, there would have been a pleasingly tight connection to Genesis 37:2, which reads: 'These are the descendants (*tōledôt*) of Jacob.' It would also have resulted, tidily, in a list of twelve generations.

As it is, the list spans ten generations, which might possibly be a deliberate echo of the ten years of barrenness experienced by Naomi and her daughters-in-law between the death of Elimelech and the deaths of Mahlon and Chilion specified in the prologue (1:4) – although it has to be acknowledged that ten generation genealogies in the Hebrew scriptures are familiar enough (Adam to Noah in Genesis 5; Noah to Abraham in Genesis 11). In addition, because the list starts with Perez, Boaz is placed seventh, perhaps signifying completeness and perfection, rather as Enoch is placed in the genealogy in the list of Adam's descendants in Genesis 5. The same ten names representing ten generations are recorded in the same sequence in 1 Chronicles 2:5–15 (though Salmon is recorded as Salma): that genealogy is only longer because it is not simply linear. The one in this epilogue has no interest in the siblings of those named or in their descendants.

For most readers of the book of Ruth, it is undeniably jarring that a narrative which has focused mostly on the agency and perspective of its female characters ends with a patrilineal genealogy. Arguably even more jarring, given the irreducibly patriarchal world of the Hebrew scriptures, is the absence from this list of Mahlon or Elimelech, possibly also Chilion, whose names the birth of Obed was expected to secure (see 4:5, 10). This omission is odd not least because this act serves as a parallel to Act I, where their names are prominent.

Two observations are in order by way of mitigation.

The first is that the Hebrew word which the NRSV rather unhelpfully translates 'became the father of' is in fact as capable of being applied to a mother as a father (as, for example, in Genesis 4:1, Numbers 26:59, and Judges 13:24). The word is *hôlîd*, from the root *yalad*. Applied to a woman, it is generally translated 'gave birth to'. Here a more fitting (ungendered) translation would simply be 'brought forth'. The significance of this gender-neutral word is further diluted in the NRSV by its decision, to prevent the genealogy becoming numbingly repetitive, to translate it just once, in verse 18. In the Hebrew it occurs nine times (in each place where the NRSV has 'of').

The second is that the genealogy serves to reiterate points made in the previous act, by the repetition of the first and last names in the list. In the process, Ruth's status is (admittedly subtly) reinforced: the reader is again reminded, by the reference to Perez, that Ruth is a latter-day Tamar and, by the reference to David, that she became the great-grandmother of Israel's greatest king. There can be little doubt that, for the earliest readers and hearers of the text, the final word of the book (David) served as a resounding climax, not a disappointing anticlimax, underlining Ruth's significance rather than rendering her invisible. The veiled reference to Israel's kings may also serve as a final point of literary symmetry in the book, complementing the reference to the Judges in 1:1. The effect is to underline for the audience Ruth's extraordinary contribution, as a migrant from Moab fully integrated into Israel, to the future life of the people of God.

A second genealogy, in which Ruth's name is present: Matthew 1:1–17

[1]An account of the genealogy of Jesus the Messiah, the son of David, the son of Abraham.

[2]Abraham was the father of Isaac, and Isaac the father of Jacob, and Jacob the father of Judah and his brothers, [3]and Judah the father of Perez and Zerah by Tamar, and Perez the father of Hezron, and Hezron the father of Aram, [4]and Aram the father of Aminadab, and Aminadab the father of Nahshon, and Nahshon the father of Salmon, [5]and Salmon the father of Boaz by Rahab, and Boaz the father of Obed by Ruth, and Obed the father of Jesse, [6]and Jesse the father of King David.

And David was the father of Solomon by the wife of Uriah, [7]and Solomon the father of Rehoboam, and Rehoboam the father of Abijah, and Abijah the father of Asaph, [8]and Asaph the father of Jehoshaphat, and Jehoshaphat the father of Joram, and Joram the father of Uzziah, [9]and Uzziah the father of Jotham, and Jotham the father of Ahaz, and Ahaz the father of Hezekiah, [10]and

Hezekiah the father of Manasseh, and Manasseh the father of Amos, and Amos the father of Josiah, [11]and Josiah the father of Jechoniah and his brothers, at the time of the deportation to Babylon.

[12]And after the deportation to Babylon: Jechoniah was the father of Salathiel, and Salathiel the father of Zerubbabel, [13]and Zerubbabel the father of Abiud, and Abiud the father of Eliakim, and Eliakim the father of Azor, [14]and Azor the father of Zadok, and Zadok the father of Achim, and Achim the father of Eliud, [15]and Eliud the father of Eleazar, and Eleazar the father of Matthan, and Matthan the father of Jacob, [16]and Jacob the father of Joseph the husband of Mary, of whom Jesus was born, who is called the Messiah.

[17]So all the generations from Abraham to David are fourteen generations; and from David to the deportation to Babylon, fourteen generations; and from the deportation to Babylon to the Messiah, fourteen generations.

MATTHEW 1:1–17

For Christian readers, it is striking that these two women, Tamar (verse 3) and Ruth (verse 5), reappear in the genealogy which occupies the first 17 verses of Matthew 1. At first sight this genealogy sounds like a list of the great and the good. It sounds like an attempt to establish Jesus' credibility, his noble lineage. It begins, after all, like this: 'An account of the genealogy of Jesus the Messiah, the son of David, the son of Abraham.' Even those who aren't very familiar with the Bible have generally heard of King David and Father Abraham: one, Israel's greatest sovereign, and the other, its founding ancestor. Even if they are frankly a bit sketchy about the details, many readers and hearers recognise some of the other names in that list: Isaac, Jacob, and Solomon perhaps, and then Joseph, of course, 'the husband of Mary, of whom was born Jesus, called the Messiah'. At first sight, this appears to be a list of fine, upstanding Jewish men: what a glorious line for Jesus to be born into, what a heritage.

But Matthew was altogether a more skilful and subtle, and a more subversive, writer than that. Those who stop and take note of the small print in this list, in particular the women who are included, as well as of the actual biographies of some of the men, will find reason to suppose that the evangelist's intention, in starting his gospel with this genealogy, was not at all to demonstrate that Jesus was born into a glorious line. It was almost the complete opposite.

To put it another way: what Matthew provides in his genealogy, his long list of names, is a skeleton. To understand its meaning, we need to clothe the names in flesh and blood – and it turns out there is plenty of both flesh and blood in this list. And perhaps that is Matthew's point: much as it matters to Matthew that Jesus was born into Israel's royal house, it also matters to him to show us the Lord was born into a family line full of flesh and blood, of sex and violence. He was born precisely into the mess of our world, and the mess of our own lives, in order to be its Saviour.

In clothing this skeleton with flesh and blood, let's begin with the flesh, the sex – and to the five women in the list. Of course, at the climax of the five is Mary, in verse 16, 'of whom Jesus was born, who is called the Messiah'. In the few verses that follow, Matthew is at pains to protect Mary from any hint of sexual impropriety: he recounts how Mary became pregnant before she and Joseph lived together, and how her condition was such a scandal to her husband that he proposed to divorce her quietly, to protect her from public disgrace, and had to be persuaded by the visitation of an angel to proceed with the marriage. And Ruth, too, as we have seen, just about emerges from the story with her reputation for sexual innocence intact – but only just. The same cannot be said for the other three women in the list. Tamar (to repeat) seduced her father-in-law by pretending to be a prostitute, while Rahab (in Joshua 2) really was one. And Bathsheba (though almost certainly coerced into adultery by king David) conceived Solomon out of wedlock, which is why Matthew scrupulously refers to her in verse 6 as the wife of Uriah the Hittite. So this genealogy isn't the squeaky clean and noble line it appears to be.

If there is sex in this genealogy, there is also plenty of violence. If the flesh in the list is associated especially with the women in it, the blood is associated with the men. After all, Judah (verse 3) was one of the brothers who (out of jealousy) sold Joseph into slavery. King David not only took another man's wife, but then arranged for that man to be murdered so that he could marry the widow. Solomon subjected the people of Israel to slavery in order to build his temple and palace. In fact, of the 14 kings who reigned over the kingdom of Judah from the time of David to the time of the exile, eight died violent deaths and eleven had blood on their hands. And that's just based on the information available to us in scripture.

What's the point? Is it that Matthew's genealogy isn't a list of the great and the good after all? Far from it. The evangelist isn't trying to dazzle us with the rarified nobility of Jesus' line. He's trying to impress on us, rather, that Jesus was born into a line riddled with the sins of the flesh – with the mess of untidy relationships, family dysfunction, and unwholesome sex. He's trying to impress on us that Jesus was born not into tidy respectability, but into a bloody line, a family of cheats, liars, murderers, and assassins, with more than its fair share of intrigue and tragedy.

And, of course, Matthew will go on, in the rest of his gospel, to emphasise that in his life and death, Jesus associated not with the great and the good, but with the despised, the marginalised, and the stigmatised, with refugees and asylum seekers. He did it because (as he said himself) it is not the well who need a doctor, but the sick; he came 'to call not the righteous but sinners to repentance' (see Luke 5:31–32). Matthew's point is that Jesus came from a line of sinners, to save his people from their sins.

Ana Maria's story

to Sheffield from Chile

Like Victor's story, which began this series of testimonies from contemporary migrants, Ana Maria's story is mature. She reflects back over a 50-year period on her transition from crisis and calamity, to migration and kinship, to subsistence and vulnerability, to security and wellbeing, to integration and inheritance, and finally to contribution and legacy.

I am now 79 years old and I have been in England for over 50 years, but I am originally from Chile. I left there in 1975, because of the terrible military dictatorship led by General Augusto Pinochet, who seized power in 1973. Over the course of the next 17 years, his regime exercised a cruel oppression: thousands of people were killed or disappeared, and tens of thousands were detained and tortured.

I was raised in the south of Chile, where my father was a dentist, who also had a healthcare role in the service of Allende's socialist government. So following the military coup, my father was placed under house arrest. At that time I was finishing my degree in biochemistry. The universities were a key focus of opposition to Pinochet, and in the first year of the dictatorship I saw friends and colleagues put in prison and tortured. My fiancé disappeared. Hundreds of people, and especially young people, were leaving the country in trauma. Almost every family had someone who disappeared, was tortured, or was imprisoned. So my father advised me to flee. This was a distressing decision, because I was an only child. But it was clear there was no prospect for me to have a good career in Chile.

So in 1974 I flew to Madrid with one suitcase. I had not even had time to say farewell to my loved ones. I was 28 years old. There was a professor at the university in Madrid with an international reputation in the field of study I was working in, so I approached him and he arranged for me to have a bursary to do some research for one year. Then I wanted to enrol for a PhD. That wasn't possible in Madrid, but with the help of this professor I secured a place to study in London with a professor at Middlesex Hospital on a British Council bursary.

At first, I was put in a hotel for refugees. I lived there for about two months, but shortly after I met a friend who put me up in his house in Islington. I stayed there for the rest of my time in London – from 1975 to 1989, 14 years in all. Much of that time is a blur; many of us were suffering nightmares because of the horrors we had experienced. It took me the best part of ten years to come to terms with what had happened, and even so I am still scarred by it now. There was a lot of despair and anguish in my generation of refugees, mainly because we knew that the country we remembered no longer existed and that we couldn't go back to a job or to study or to be the same person we once were.

In 1979, my father came to London to say goodbye. His health had deteriorated and he died later the same year. I was not able to attend his funeral; it would not have been safe to return to Chile at that time.

In the early 1980s, I formed a relationship with a civil servant, Robert, who had moved into the flat in Islington. In 1983, our son Thomas was born, and in 1985 I completed my PhD.

Towards the end of the 1980s, many things changed. Robert was transferred by the civil service to Sheffield, and Thomas and I went with him, leaving behind the large Chilean community in London. From 1988, I gained a British passport, acquiring dual citizenship. Then in 1989, Pinochet was overthrown, opening up the prospect that I might return to Chile. Many refugees and exiles did return at that time. I visited with Thomas, and I did consider settling in Chile again. But Robert missed us and urged us to return, so we did.

Robert and I separated in 1991. By then I had found work at the University of Sheffield, where I was employed to set up a lab, working in the field of diabetes. I had a good career there, retiring in 2009. I grew tired of applying for grants from charities which might benefit from our research, in order to pay my own salary. In fact, for a short time, when Thomas was a teenager, I got a good job back in London. Thomas lived with his father in the week and came to see me at the weekends. But that didn't work and his school urged me to give him more continuity, so I took voluntary redundancy and came back to Sheffield.

These days it is safe for me to visit Chile and I go each year to meet up with the friends I had before the dictatorship, friends from university, school, and even from nursery! Each time I leave Chile, I cry. My mother died in 2014, and this time I was able to attend the funeral.

But even though I enjoyed a good career in England, these past 50 years have been hard. Although I hold a British passport, I don't always feel very British; but when I go to Chile, I don't feel Chilean either. My parenting style is an example of the clash of cultures. In Chile, we like colourful things because of the sun and because of the happiness of the people. So I used to dress Thomas in bright colours, and people used to criticise this, including Robert's mother. As a boy, Thomas wore a ponytail. In South America this is quite common, but it wasn't here at that time. So we didn't always feel as if we belonged here.

Now my life has two chief joys.

The first is Thomas, who still lives in Sheffield. We are close and go to watch football (Sheffield United!) together. I keep reminding Thomas he is half and half: 50% British and 50% Chilean – but he hasn't been back to Chile since he was nine years old. I will never leave the UK now, because of him.

My second joy is to volunteer in support of refugees and asylum seekers, especially at present from Iran, Pakistan, and parts of Africa. I have never forgotten what it is like to be a refugee. My hope for the future is that some new government policies will help asylum seekers come into this country with the right to work. That is so important for them and that's my big hope really. The recent riots and demonstrations against asylum seekers and refugees have shocked me.

Conclusion

Blessing and kindness in the book of Ruth – and its implications for the treatment of migrants today

O ne of the distinctive features of the book of Ruth is the extent to which all its characters act with kindness and generosity towards one another. It may only be Boaz (2:1) and Ruth (3:11) who are explicitly described as virtuous or noble (*chayil*), but in practice they share this quality with the whole Bethlehem community (which may account for the prayer of its womenfolk that the union of Boaz and Ruth will issue in *chayil* in Ephrathah, 4:11). Why is this? The behaviour of these citizens of Bethlehem is not presented as a matter of chance. These characters are not coincidentally good and kind. Their ethics are not independent of their faith; their behaviour is not unrelated to their knowledge of the LORD. On the contrary, the character of the *dramatis personae* in the book of Ruth is derived directly from the character of the LORD in whom they have put their trust. It is a theological truism that human beings are shaped by the nature of the God they worship.

That said, the book of Ruth is a rare thing among the books of the Hebrew scriptures: the LORD is somewhat in the background. There is some similarity here with the only other book in the Bible named after a woman: the book of Esther. Esther is a story about a Jewish woman living among foreigners; Ruth is about a foreign woman living among Israelites. In both books, the sovereign providence of God is at work, but in and through ordinary men and women living out their ordinary lives. The hand of God is rather veiled, and the voice of God is silent. In Esther, there is not one single reference to God – not by any name. God doesn't directly act or speak and is not once worshipped or acknowledged, though the audience discerns his presence all the same. The LORD also seldom acts, and never speaks, in the book of Ruth. But unlike in Esther, in the book of Ruth there are numerous references to the LORD, 18 in all, and these arguably turn out to be key to an adequate understanding of the book.

References to the LORD in the Hebrew scriptures

A word of explanation may be helpful to some readers at this point. When an English Bible translation prints 'LORD' (with an initial capital letter, followed by small capitals), as in Ruth 1:6, it is translating a very particular Hebrew word, *Yahweh*, which (to this day) Jewish people have regarded as too sacred to be spoken out loud. This is the 'personal' name by which God made himself known to Israel (for example, Exodus 3:13–15; 6:2–8). The implications of this name are spelt out most fully and definitively in Exodus 34:6, when the LORD descended on Mount Sinai in a cloud and stood there with Moses, and proclaimed the name: 'The LORD, the LORD, a God merciful and gracious, slow to anger and abounding in steadfast love [*hesed*] and faithfulness.' (These words are repeated almost exactly – and always including that word *hesed* – in Nehemiah 9:17; Psalm 86:15; 103:8; 145:8; Joel 2:13; Jonah 4:2.) So 'the LORD' becomes, in the Hebrew scriptures, a sort of short-hand for 'the God of covenant faithfulness' or 'the God of steadfast love' or indeed 'the God of kindness' – and by extension, 'the God of Israel'.

When we encounter 'lord' in an English Bible translation referring to a human being (as in Ruth 2:13), it renders a completely different Hebrew word, *adonai*, which means master. Of course, this word can also refer to God (though it doesn't in the book of Ruth); in such instances English translations usually put 'Lord' (in lower case with an initial capital, as in Exodus 34:9). A third Hebrew word, *Elohim*, is a rather generic term, simply translated 'God' in English Bibles (as in Ruth 1:16; 2:12). This word has parallels in other Middle Eastern languages, so it sounds not unlike Allah, for example.

Finally, to complicate things a little, in the Hebrew scriptures we often meet two compound names for God, *Yahweh Elohim* and *Adonai Yahweh*, though neither of these occurs in the book of Ruth. The former is usually translated as 'LORD God' (as in Genesis 2—3); but for the latter (which occurs frequently in Ezekiel and Amos), in order to avoid the clumsy 'Lord LORD', most English translations prefer 'Lord GOD' or 'Sovereign LORD', again with the second word capitalised to indicate the Hebrew *Yahweh*.

The decision to print 'LORD' in (most) English Bibles is therefore a mark of respect for the ancient Hebrew tradition, but also the contemporary Jewish custom, to not pronounce this sacred name. Given the extreme preciousness of this name for God in the Hebrew scriptures (the one observant Jews tend to call *Ha Shem*, The Name), it is as well to be attentive to it when it occurs.

References to the LORD in the book of Ruth

In the book of Ruth references to the LORD turn out to have a programmatic significance. This is already indicated by the fact that an appeal to the LORD is made in every chapter of the book (and in four of the six parts of the chiasm, with the symmetrical exceptions of the prologue and the epilogue) and by each of the three main individuals in the cast list: by Naomi (1:8, 9, 13, 21 [x2]; 2:20); Ruth (1:17); and Boaz (2:4, 12 [x2]; 3:10, 13). Moreover, an appeal to the LORD is made also by each of the three identifiable groups within the Bethlehem community: by the harvesters (2:4); the people and elders of the town (4:11, 12); and the women (4:14). (Although the narrative invites no real criticism of either Orpah or the anonymous next-of-kin for the decisions they make in relation to Naomi, it is probably significant that there are no equivalent appeals to the LORD on their lips.)

It is also noteworthy that the vast majority of these 18 references to the LORD occur in sections of dialogue. The significance of this is explored further below. The two exceptions were noted at the relevant points in the exposition. One comes right at the beginning of Act I (1:6) and the other close to the end of Act IV (4:13). In both cases, the narrator regards the LORD as the author of fertility: first in visiting his people to provide them with bread, and then in enabling Ruth to conceive a son. These are also the only two occasions in the book of Ruth when the action of God is reported. Even so, in the first case the reference is to a rumour in Moab of what God has done 'off-stage' in Bethlehem. In the book of Ruth, then, the direct work of God is barely evident, but it still hints at blessing and kindness where it is to be found. The vast majority of the other references to the LORD, the ones which occur in the sections of dialogue, fill out this impression.

It transpires that just as the LORD doesn't speak in the book of Ruth, so none of the characters speak to the LORD as such; instead, they all speak to others about the LORD. Yet, almost without exception, these references to the LORD are still best characterised as 'prayers': in almost every case they are wishes, spoken by one of the characters in the story to another, about what they hope the LORD will do. By and large, these are benedictions, calling down the blessing of God upon another person.

Exceptions to the general pattern of references to the LORD in the book of Ruth

Admittedly, five of the 16 references to the LORD which are to be found in sections of dialogue do not quite fit this pattern.

In three cases (none of them in any sense prayers), the references to the LORD are darker. It is no coincidence that all three occur in Act I, in which the narrative is also at its darkest, and on the lips of Naomi, whose life experience has been bitter. First, in speaking to her two daughters-in-law, she asserts that 'the hand of the LORD has turned against me' (1:13). Then, in speaking to the women of Bethlehem, she tells them that 'I went away full, but the LORD has brought me back empty… the LORD has dealt harshly with me' (1:21). Obviously, there is no faith being expressed here in a God of kindness and blessing. And yet these utterances remain confessions of faith: Naomi's knowledge of the LORD is such that she perceives herself to be in God's hands, for good or ill. The LORD remains the LORD, and remains her LORD, even in the depths of adversity. These confessions of faith have the virtue of being true to Naomi's experience: she does not pretend that her situation is better than it is or that her experience of God has been more positive than it has. Naomi's faith is viscerally realistic and honest. In this regard, she is in good company with other figures in the Hebrew scriptures who have dared to protest to God or about God – among them most obviously Job (notably in Job 10), Jeremiah (most vehemently in Jeremiah 20:7–9, 14–18), and the psalmist (most relentlessly in Psalms 44 and 88).

The other two exceptions are references to the LORD in the context of oath-making. First, in Act I at the climax of her great affirmation of loyalty to Naomi, Ruth concludes: 'May the LORD do thus and so to me, and more as well, if even death parts me from you!' (1:17). This is a good example of what is meant by a 'wish-prayer'. The LORD is not spoken to here but is only spoken of, not addressed in the second person but referred to in the third. Yet Ruth is clearly expressing an expectation that the LORD will act in response to her words. 'Thus and so' is an invitation to the audience to insert its own imprecation: Ruth expects severe, if unspecified, treatment from the LORD if she proves untrue to Naomi. So this reference to the LORD is also slightly sinister. Nevertheless, it too remains a confession of faith: Ruth is doubling down on her pledge to take Naomi's God as her own God. The other oath comes in Act III. At the end of his speech to Ruth on the threshing-floor, Boaz similarly swears with reference to the LORD, promising to act promptly to resolve her situation. He will do so 'as the LORD lives' (3:13). This may be less obviously a wish-prayer, but the oath only has force on the assumption that the LORD who lives will act if Boaz fails to do what he is promising to do.

The Lord of blessing and kindness

Of the other eleven references to the Lord in the book of Ruth that occur in sections of dialogue, ten consistently also share two other features: they are wish-prayers, and they assume the Lord to be a God of blessing and kindness The remaining reference happens to be the very last one in the book. Although it does not share both the other features, this verse (4:14) does constitute an appropriately climactic conclusion to the series as a whole.

The first two of these references come early in Act I, in 1:8–9, when (on the road to Bethlehem from Moab) Naomi urges her two daughters-in-law to go back each to their mother's house. Her words are unmistakably a petition: 'May the Lord deal kindly [*hesed*] with you, as you have dealt with the dead and with me.' As well as being the first such wish-prayer in the story, this is the first of three highly significant occurrences of the Hebrew word *hesed* (the others come at 2:20 and 3:10, see below). *Hesed* is a difficult word to translate satisfactorily into English. It is often rendered 'covenant loyalty' or 'steadfast love'. But in the context of the book of Ruth and not least in the context of migration, the ordinary word 'kindness' serves extremely well. Naomi is acknowledging the kindness she has received from Orpah and Ruth, and which they also showed previously to Chilion and Mahlon (and possibly also to Elimelech, or at least to his memory). In effect, she is praying that as they return to their Moab-lives (and in return for their kindness) her daughters-in-law will know the kindness of the Lord. She amplifies this wish when she goes on: 'The Lord grant that you may find security, each of you in the house of your husband.' Naomi knows the Lord to be the source of security, and longs for him to give it to her two daughters-in-law.

There is then a further pair of references to the Lord early in Act II, in 2:4. As Boaz arrives in his field, he greets his workers with the words, 'The Lord be with you.' Immediately the reply comes back, 'The Lord bless you.' This exchange receives some attention in the exposition earlier (see page 58). Here it is sufficient to note that these brief greetings (each just two words long in the Hebrew) share the general pattern: they are pieces of dialogue, they wish for the LORD to act in particular ways, and they assume the LORD to be a source of kindness and blessing.

The same is true of the next two references, both spoken by Boaz to Ruth later in Act II, in 2:12. He has heard about all that she has done for Naomi since the death of Mahlon, and now expresses his wish for her: 'May the LORD reward you for your deeds, and may you have a full reward from the LORD, the God of Israel, under whose wings you have come for refuge!' Where the NRSV twice puts 'reward', the Hebrew uses two different words. In the first case, a more helpful translation might be 'May the LORD repay you'. In any case, we again find sentiments which are unquestionably petitions for God to act in blessing.

There is arguably one more pair of examples at the end of Act II, in 2:19–20, even if the name of the LORD is only used once. When Ruth returns to Naomi at the end of her day of gleaning, and Naomi hears how well she has fared, she cries out, 'Blessed be the man who took notice of you.' That she expects this blessing to issue from none other than the LORD is clarified in the following verse, after she has learned that the man in question is Boaz: 'Blessed be he by the LORD, whose kindness [*hesed*] has not forsaken the living or the dead.' Commentators are agreed that there is an ambiguity here. To which of the two possible antecedents does the word 'whose' belong? Is the kindness celebrated here, which has not forsaken the living or the dead, the kindness of Boaz or the kindness of the LORD? The ambiguity may be deliberate, and the answer may be both. Again, as in 1:8, it is worth noting that the kindness in view has been shown towards the living (Naomi and Ruth) and the dead (Elimelech, Mahlon, and Chilion) – or at least towards their memory.

The next example also fits the pattern perfectly. In Act III, in 3:10, Boaz suddenly awakes on the threshing-floor at midnight to discover a woman lying at his uncovered feet. When he realises it is none other than Ruth, who pleads with him to spread his cloak over her and to act as her next-of-kin, he exclaims, 'May you be blessed by the LORD, my daughter; this last instance of your loyalty [*hesed*] is better than the first' (3:10). The latest instance of Ruth's kindness has been to seek a covenant relationship with Boaz, rather than chasing after younger men. According to Boaz, this act compares favourably with her 'first' act of kindness, which was presumably to commit herself to Naomi and to an uncertain future as a migrant in Bethlehem, when she might have preferred to remain in Moab, with all its familiar structures of support. For such kindness, Boaz prays that Ruth will be 'blessed by the LORD'.

There is then a final pair of references to the LORD in Act IV, in 4:11–12 (on the lips of 'all the people who were at the gate, along with the elders'). At the conclusion of the transaction by which Boaz acquired all that belonged to Elimelech, Chilion, and Mahlon, and also acquired Ruth the Moabite to be his wife, they cried out: 'May the LORD make the woman who is coming into your house like Rachel and Leah... through the children that the LORD will give you by this young woman, may your house be like the house of Perez, whom Tamar bore to Judah.' Again we meet the same pattern: the LORD is invoked in dialogue and a wish is expressed which (even if the exact vocabulary is not there) assumes the LORD to be a God of blessing and kindness.

The neat pattern at first sight breaks down in relation to the very last reference to the LORD in the book of Ruth, in 4:14. The context is, once more, a piece of dialogue – but there is no petition, no wish expressed. Rather, when the women hear that Ruth has given birth to a son, they rejoice with Naomi, saying, 'Blessed be the LORD, who has not left you this day without next-of-kin.' Here then the LORD is blessed, rather than invoked as a source of blessing. But the LORD is blessed precisely on account of the blessing he has poured out upon Naomi through the birth of Ruth's son, so that she has not been left without a next-of-kin. Commonly in the Hebrew scriptures, the LORD is blessed in acknowledgement of his blessings; he is thanked for the gifts he has given. So this final reference to the LORD in the book of Ruth may reasonably be taken as an apt conclusion to the series.

Kindness in community in the book of Ruth

Together these ten references (1:8, 9; 2:4 [x2], 12 [x2], 20; 3:10; 4:11, 12) constitute a consistent and comprehensive pattern. The pattern is consistent in that each reference is set in dialogue, amounts to a prayer for the LORD to act in a certain way, and assumes the LORD to be a God of kindness and blessing. It is comprehensive in that the pattern is to be found in all four acts of the drama and embraces not only each of the three major individual players (Naomi, Ruth, and Boaz), but also each of the three identifiable groups within Bethlehem (the harvesters, the elders, and the women).

Together, the consistency and the comprehensiveness indicate that something normative is in view: here is a community which acknowledges the LORD with its lips and seeks to honour him with its common life. The knowledge of God is sufficiently embedded in this community for its members to speak easily of him to one another; his name comes readily and sincerely to their lips. And the knowledge of God is sufficiently embedded in this community for its members instinctively to imitate him in the way they relate to one another. Since they know the LORD to be gracious and merciful, they relate to one another in ways which are gracious and merciful. Since they know the LORD to be slow to anger and abounding in steadfast love [*hesed*], they relate to one another in kindness. Indeed, so formed are they by their knowledge of the LORD, that they even relate to the outsider, the migrant, with kindness.

Ultimately, the book of Ruth is not actually about Ruth and Naomi. It is not even about their wider community, comprising Boaz and his workers, the elders, the women, and all the people of Bethlehem. For all that he never speaks and barely acts directly, this is a story about their LORD. If Ruth and Naomi, Boaz and the people of Bethlehem turn out to be noble people, who act in ways that are generous and kind, it is because their character reflects the character of the LORD they have known. This interplay between divine and human kindness is nicely illustrated by the ambiguity in Naomi's words in 2:20. We have noted already that when she says, 'Blessed be he by the LORD, whose kindness [*hesed*] has not forsaken the living or the dead', it is not clear whose kindness she means, whether the kindness of the LORD or the kindness of Boaz. Part of the point might be precisely that the latter derives from the former. That interplay of divine and human kindness is even more clear in 1:8.

If the book of Ruth can be described as a study in kindness, this is why: it is because the book explores what human community can look like when it is shaped by the nature of God. The persistent kindness of the people of Bethlehem in this story is all the more impressive because it is set in the time of the judges (1:1), when kindness was in short supply. But then, at the time of the judges, people 'did not know the LORD' (Judges 2:10).

Kindness and refuge for migrants today

In its *World Migration Report* for 2022, the United Nations International Organization for Migration (IOM) states its commitment 'to the principle that humane and orderly migration benefits migrants and society. As an intergovernmental organization, IOM acts with its partners in the international community to: assist in meeting the operational challenges of migration; advance understanding of migration issues; encourage social and economic development through migration; and uphold the human dignity and well-being of migrants.'[7]

It goes without saying that every national government is responsible for framing policy in relation to migration, and government policies are bound to vary according to time, place, and circumstance. However, the challenging commitment of the IOM expressed here combines at least two elements, which every government will surely wish to weigh carefully in the formulation of migration policy: the right of migrants to be treated humanely (to experience kindness), on the one hand, and the potential of migrants to benefit both society and themselves, on the other. So the IOM seeks to 'encourage social and economic development through migration', on the one hand, and to 'uphold the human dignity and well-being of migrants', on the other. This vision for global migration is a long way from a hostile environment.

Both these elements are combined in the book of Ruth. The experience of Ruth and Naomi might almost be considered a case-study to illustrate the commitment of the IOM. As the kindness and blessing of God were mediated to them by the people of Bethlehem, and pre-eminently by Boaz (as they were treated humanely), they were enabled to move from crisis and calamity, as safely as possible through migration and kinship, subsistence and vulnerability, to security and wellbeing. In making this journey, and in finding integration and inheritance, they made a contribution and left a legacy, so benefiting not only themselves but their place of refuge. This is a journey every forced migrant aspires to make, and it is kindness which enables it.

This is precisely the point of the 'happy ending' in the book of Ruth, at the conclusion of Act IV: 'So Boaz took Ruth and she became his wife. When they came together, the LORD made her conceive, and she bore a son… The women of the neighbourhood gave him a name, saying, "A son has been born to Naomi." They named him Obed; he became the father of Jesse, the father of David.' In the providence of God, the legacy of this migrant woman to the society in which she sought refuge was nothing less than the grandfather of Israel's greatest king. The story invites the audience to ask what might have been lost if she had not received sanctuary in Israel. A contemporary British reader might be tempted to consider how things would have turned out if Israel had set out to 'stop the boats'. A hostile environment runs the risk of rendering a country Ruth-less.

One final thought: the practice of kindness is not without risk. When Boaz found Ruth at his feet on the threshing-floor, he commended her for her kindness, saying, 'May you be blessed by the LORD, my daughter; this last instance of your loyalty [hesed] is better than the first' (3:10). The first instance of Ruth's kindness was presumably the choice she made to go with Naomi as a migrant to Bethlehem – it was an action full of risk, with the outcome uncertain. This was all the more true of the last instance of her loyalty, in propositioning Boaz: it was an action full of risk, with the outcome uncertain. Arguably, the repeated acts of kindness shown by Boaz to Ruth (and so also to Naomi) in Act II were also risky: when he not only permitted her for one day to glean among his young women and ensured she would not be pestered by his young men (2:9), but also permitted her to drink from water than his harvesters had drawn (2:9), and then invited her to join him for a midday meal (2:14), and then also ensured her gleanings were enriched (2:16). Boaz's kindness was risky, at least in the sense that others might easily have resented his generosity to this migrant woman, this outsider.

That too is precisely the point: it is in the nature of kindness (and especially kindness to the migrant, the refugee, the outsider) to be courageous and even risky. Perhaps it is in the LORD's nature, also.

Study session six

Participants are invited to prepare by reading, pages 110–131.

No additional resources are necessary for this session. You may need to factor in additional time to make good farewells at the end or to plan next steps.

Welcome (15 minutes)

Each group member is invited to respond to these questions:

- What is the most important thing which has happened to you in the past week?
- What have you found most valuable about *Come for Refuge*?
- What have you found most frustrating about *Come for Refuge*?
- Who is your hero (female or male) in life in general?
- What is it about this person that you find inspiring?
- Is there something you'd really like to do before you die?

The facilitator may like to lead an opening prayer, committing to God the discussion and reflection which follows.

Word (40 minutes)

Before reading the short Bible text together, allow 20 minutes to reflect together:

- What do you know about your own family tree?
- How many generations of your forebears are you familiar with?
- What do you hope your legacy might be?

- What would you expect the contribution of a refugee in your community to be?

Read the Bible text together: Ruth 4:18–22 (20 minutes).

(Brave participants may also like to read Matthew 1:1–17!)

- Do these verses feel to you like a climax or an anti-climax?
- How far do you think your response to these verses is a cultural one?
- What did you make of Matthew's use of the genealogy from Ruth?
- Was there material in the exposition which sparked a new thought?

Work (20 minutes)

- Among her many troubles, Ana Maria says simply that 'My fiancé disappeared'. Almost every refugee testimony includes great suffering. What risks do you think might be involved if a refugee chooses to express their pain fully, and what risks might be involved if a refugee chooses to understate it?
- Like many asylum seekers, Ana Maria is highly qualified. Yet in many countries there are significant limits on asylum seekers being able to work, despite evidence that it would benefit the economy. What do you think about this?
- The conclusion (pages 125–129) focuses in on 'kindness' as a key value in the book of Ruth. What do you think kindness to migrants means in practice?
- The conclusion (pages 129–131) describes an essentially positive attitude towards global migration. Do you find it convincing or concerning?
- What have you learned from *Come for Refuge* about the role of the local church in relation to migrants, refugees, and asylum seekers?

Worship (5 minutes)

As this six-week engagement with the book of Ruth and global migration comes to a conclusion, it is appropriate to end in worship with the emphasis on gratitude:

- For all the privileges of life in a settled society: for food and shelter, health and wealth, political stability and freedom from war.
- For all that refugees and asylum seekers contribute to our society.
- For the gift of holy scripture and for our fellowship in Jesus Christ.

If you have capacity

Why not acquaint yourself with the basic facts about asylum in your country and try gently to dispel misinformation when you encounter it? For example: the UK receives considerably fewer asylum applications than Germany, France, Spain, or Italy. The number of people arriving by small boat each year is a small fraction (around 6% at the time of publication) of those who come legally to work and study.

Guide to study materials

E ach study session is material offered to support small groups who wish to study the book of Ruth and/or to engage with the issue of migration, using the text of *Come for Refuge* as a basic resource. Below provides a summary of how this study material is best used.

The material supports six sessions of 60–90 minutes – the amount of time required will depend on several factors, including the number of people in the group. The material has been prepared on the assumption that groups are gathering onsite rather than online, but only slight adaptation will be necessary for groups which gather remotely. Care has been taken to ensure that the study materials, and especially the resources for worship, are accessible and inclusive, but group leaders may need to make modest adaptations in view of the particular needs of group members.

The material assumes that each week group members will have read not only the relevant part of the biblical text, but also the relevant exposition and the accompanying contemporary migrant testimony from *Come for Refuge*.

Each session follows the same four-part structure:

Welcome: to allow group members to get to know one another or to catch up on developments in one another's lives through the period of the group's meetings.

Word: the heart of each session, to enable group members to engage with the biblical text and the exposition in *Come for Refuge* and to set their own experience of life beside it.

Work: which seeks to raise awareness about contemporary issues in relation to migrants and refugees and to give participants the opportunity to consider their own responses.

Worship: to conclude the session in prayer and reflection, offering all that has been thought and said and done to the Almighty, the only refuge.

If additional resources are required for the suggested activities, these are listed for each session.

The material assumes that the small group includes a facilitator. This person is not expected to be a resident Bible or migration expert, but to assist each member of the group in engaging with the material and the other participants fully, drawing out the quietest members and quietening the most vocal. A key priority for the facilitator is to ensure the group keeps roughly to time and certainly finishes on schedule. The facilitator is encouraged to share out the other roles, such as the leading of the brief act of worship each week.

Acknowledgements

I t is beyond question that the book of Ruth took shape over time, almost certainly at first in an oral culture as a spoken tale. It wasn't written by a single author in a single sitting. But the form it now has it has had for at least 2,000 years, and what is offered in this commentary is a reading of this text in this form. My exposition of the book of Ruth offers nothing in the way of interaction with other interpreters of the text or (explicitly, at least) with current academic scholarship. But where I comment on the Hebrew text, my observations are generally derived from the insights of others.

Those who wish to explore questions such as the textual history of Ruth, its composition, date, original historical setting, sources, and parallels are referred to the many excellent commentaries which exist. In generating my own exposition, I have especially valued the chance to read the volumes by Daniel I. Block (New American Commentary); F. Bush (Word); Peter H. W. Lau (New International Commentary on the Old Testament); Karen Lawson Younger (New International Version Application Commentary); Katharine Sakenfield (Interpretation); Kirsten Neilsen (Old Testament Library); and Robert L. Hubbard Jr (New International Commentary on the Old Testament). I was challenged by my reading of *Losing Ground: Reading Ruth in the Pacific* by Jione Havea (SCM Press, 2021) and of *Borders and Belonging: The book of Ruth: A story for our times* by Pádraig Ó Tuama and Glenn Jordan (Canterbury Press, 2021). In the writing up of this text I stumbled gratefully upon Kelly Dagley's PhD thesis, 'Women's experience of migration and the book of Ruth'. Readers who know these works will doubtless discern my indebtedness, which I am glad to acknowledge.

Much of the work on this book was accomplished during a period of sabbatical in the first quarter of 2024. I am grateful to the Bishop's Council in the diocese of Sheffield for encouraging me to take up this opportunity, and to the Diocesan Board of Finance for a most generous grant to enable our trip to Melbourne, Australia. Senior colleagues in the diocese took on additional responsibilities in my absence, and I am especially grateful to the Rt Revd Sophie Jelley (formerly the bishop of Doncaster, and now the bishop of Coventry) who became the acting bishop of Sheffield for that time.

Other grants were generously made by: the insurance company Eccle-siastical; Clergy Support Trust; Sheffield Church Burgesses Trust; St George's Trust; St Boniface Trust; and Whirlow Spirituality Centre. This support was hugely helpful in enabling the programme of travel and study I planned, and was much appreciated.

In Melbourne we met with warm hospitality, not least from repre-sentatives of the Anglican Diocese: from the Rt Revd Dr Philip Freier, archbishop of Melbourne, and his wife, Joy; the Rt Revd Dr Paul Barker, assistant bishop in the diocese of Melbourne; the Very Revd Andreas Loewe, the dean of Melbourne, and his wife, Dr Katherine Firth, head of Lisa Bellear House in the University of Melbourne; Judith Atkinson, chief executive officer of Concern Australia, and her husband, the Revd Prof Stephen Burns of Trinity College Theological School; the Revd Dr Peter Adam, vicar emeritus of St Jude's Carlton; and the Revd Canon Faraj Hannah at Holy Trinity Church, Coburg, and his wife, Ragaa. For five weeks of the sabbatical, we stayed in a guest flat at Mary McKil-lop Heritage Centre, where Sister Rita in particular took us under her wing. My sabbatical would not have been nearly so productive, nor so enjoyable, without the kind facilitations of them all.

Dilys Alam, policy advisor for home affairs in the Faith and Public Life Department of the Church of England, generously reviewed (and greatly improved) the study resources, contributing time and expertise promptly and gratuitously, 'with no hope of any reward'!

I am deeply grateful to all the migrants, refugees, and asylum seekers who agreed to meet with me and to tell me their stories. All showed me extraordinary generosity and trust. In the end, I accumulated more testimonies than I was able to include in the book, and I would like to acknowledge here the lived experience of Rania from Tunisia, Mazen from Iraq, Satvasheela from North India, Boucka from the Ivory Coast, Habib from Afghanistan, and Ahmed from Lebanon. Their stories touched me.

This book is dedicated with affection to the members of the bishop's senior staff team in the diocese of Sheffield and to the staff team at Bishopscroft, whose ready capacity for laughter is one of the chief joys of my present ministry.

Pete Wilcox

NOTES

1   IOM, *World Migration Report 2024* (IOM, 2024), **publications.iom.int/books/world-migration-report-2024**.

2   Convention relating to the Status of Refugees, **ohchr.org/en/instruments-mechanisms/instruments/convention-relating-status-refugees**.

3   IOM, 'Key migration terms', **iom.int/key-migration-terms**.

4   IOM, *IOM Institutional Strategy on Migration and Sustainable Development* (IOM, 2020), **publications.iom.int/books/iom-institutional-strategy-migration-and-sustainable-development**.

5   IOM, 'Migration and migrants: a global overview', *World Migration Report 2024* (IOM, 2024), ch. 2, **worldmigrationreport.iom.int/what-we-do/world-migration-report-2024-chapter-2/international-remittances**.

6   House of Lords, 'Impact of "Hostile Environment" Policy', **lordslibrary.parliament.uk/research-briefings/lln-2018-0064**.

7   IOM, *World Migration Report 2022*, **publications.iom.int/books/world-migration-report-2022**.

ENCOUNTERING THE DIVINE
IN THE WORKS OF MERCY

JONATHAN ARNOLD

Foreword by Rose Hudson-Wilkin, Bishop of Dover

Jonathan Arnold delves deep into the heart of the biblical mandate to love one's neighbour. Through a tapestry of real-life stories, he unveils the power of practical faith, illustrating how it can ignite transformation among the homeless, refugees, the poor and vulnerable, imprisoned and marginalised, as well as those living with dementia, disability and disease. In these pages, you'll witness how acts of social and environmental justice, intertwined with mercy, have the potential to reshape lives, offering a vivid portrait of the profound impact of embracing the everyday God. As he reflects upon Jesus's teaching in Matthew 25:34–40, Arnold challenges us to discover God's presence in the most unexpected places and join in with where God is acting, whether inside or outside our churches.

The Everyday God
Encountering the divine in the works of mercy
Jonathan Arnold
978 1 80039 210 6 £9.99

brfresources.org.uk

Few would doubt that we live in a wounded and broken world. But God has sent a Saviour, Jesus Christ, who calls us, in the beatitudes, to live an authentic, countercultural lifestyle. By being different we can make a difference, becoming the salt of the earth and the light of the world. Through living the beatitudes, we could make the world a better place.

Living Differently to Make a Difference
The beatitudes and countercultural lifestyle
Will Donaldson
978 0 85746 671 6 £8.99

brfresources.org.uk

Do you find the violence in the Old Testament a problem? Does it get in the way of reading the Bible – and of faith itself? While acknowledging that there are no easy answers, in *God of Violence Yesterday, God of Love Today?*, Helen Paynter faces the questions head-on and offers a fresh, accessible approach to a significant issue. For all those seeking to engage with the Bible and gain confidence in the God it portrays, she provides tools for reading and interpreting biblical texts, and points to ways of dealing with the overall trajectories of violence.

God of Violence Yesterday, God of Love Today?
Wrestling honestly with the Old Testament
Helen Paynter
978 0 85746 639 6 £9.99

brfresources.org.uk

BRF Ministries

Inspiring people of all ages to grow in Christian faith

BRF Ministries is the
home of Anna Chaplaincy,
BRF Resources, Messy Church
and Parenting for Faith

As a charity, our work would not be possible without
fundraising and gifts in wills.
To find out more and to donate,
visit brf.org.uk/give or call +44 (0)1865 319700

Registered with
FUNDRAISING
REGULATOR